Praise for

Raising and Teaching Children for Their Tomorrows

Al Yee was my professor as an undergraduate as I prepared to be a teacher. He inspired me and other students to be caring, dedicated educators. His book, *Raising and Teaching Children for Their Tomorrows,* is an engaging collection of research and wisdom that will inspire parents to be better parents and will motivate a future generation of teachers to make a positive difference in the lives of their students.

—Harriett Romo, PhD, Professor - Sociology/
Director of the Mexico Center, Director of the Bank
of America Child & Adolescent Policy Research
Institute, University of Texas San Antonio

Raising and Teaching Children for Their Tomorrows makes a compelling, research-based argument for the long-term effects of children's experiences early in life and the importance of good parenting and teaching. Blending unique personal stories with scientific research, the book provides sound advice for launching children on a positive life trajectory.

—Deborah Stipek, James Quillen Endowed
Dean, Stanford University School of Education

Dr. Al Yee has skillfully woven together highly relevant scholarly research findings, biographical analyses, and personal experiences in a readable text dealing with child development and parental behavior. His keen insight into the emotional socialization, learning, and creative thinking of a developing child in our ever-more complex world is indeed impressive. Any parent or teacher could profit from a careful reading of this thought-provoking book. The final chapter spells out clearly some flaws in the current American education system with suggestions on overcoming them in future policy directions.

—Wayne H. Holtzman, PhD, Hogg Professor of Psychology; former Dean, College of Education, retired President, Hogg Foundation for Mental Health, The University of Texas at Austin

My wife and I thought we were well-prepared when we had our first child, because we had read books written by famous authorities on childcare. When the second child came, we believed we were experienced parents. But when the babies started to grow, we were ill-prepared like most parents. We did our best, but we wish we had Albert Yee's book. Today's parents are fortunate to have access to this wonderful book on how to bring up their children.

Dr. Yee's book covers a wide spectrum of issues of great concern to every family with children, regardless of where they live, their social status, family composition, race, or religion. The different parenting styles are discussed in depth, and the merits of the style favored by the author are convincingly analyzed. A child's development presents challenges to parents, and the author rightfully emphasizes the importance of early education and the role of teachers. Yee's book tells why the 3-R skills and knowledge of students in other developed nations are far superior to those of U.S. students and what America must do to improve its educational system.

—Dr. George Shen, Chief Editor (ret.),
Hong Kong Economic Journal, author of
Essays on China's Economy (two volumes)
and *My Views of Japan* (in Chinese)

Raising & Teaching Children
for Their Tomorrows

To Laura
From Grt Gondma
Wiseley

Raising & Teaching Children
for Their Tomorrows

ALBERT H. YEE

Tate Publishing & Enterprises

Published by Tate Publishing & Enterprises, LLC
127 E. Trade Center Terrace | Mustang, Oklahoma 73064 USA
1.888.361.9473 | www.tatepublishing.com

Tate Publishing is committed to excellence in the publishing industry. The company reflects the philosophy established by the founders, based on Psalm 68:11,
"The Lord gave the word and great was the company of those who published it."

Book design copyright © 2011 by Tate Publishing, LLC. All rights reserved.
Cover design by Kellie Southerland
Interior design by Blake Brasor

Published in the United States of America

ISBN: 978-1-61739-212-2
Categories To be determined
10.09.19

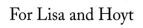
For Lisa and Hoyt

ACKNOWLEDGMENTS

I thank Dr. Henry T. Stein for granting permission to include his two charts on "Adult Consequences of Childhood Parenting Styles" in chapter three. Gratitude also goes to Ms. Kay Dorko, Library Director, Editorial Projects in Education of *Education Week,* for allowing the use of material in chapter six that "first appeared in *Education Week*'s Quality Counts 2007, reprinted with permission from Editorial Projects in Education." I also thank my friend and counsel, Mr. Dexter L. Delaney, for his encouragement and helpful reading of chapter five. Appreciation and love go to my children, the memory of their mom, and my mother, all whose care and patience have been precious.

TABLE OF CONTENTS

INTRODUCTION

Much of this book comes from my having raised children who are now successful professionals, and having taught countless elementary school pupils and university students. As a psychology and education professor for more than three decades, I sought a book with insights and findings on how and why I believe children should be raised and taught. Many of my university students told me that what I taught them about child development, teaching, and learning would be useful to them when they became parents and teachers. Failing to find the book I wanted after searching libraries and bookstores for years, I wrote *Raising and Teaching Children for Their Tomorrows* for parents, relatives, teachers, and other educators. My objective is to promote the happiness and life prospects of children.

While teaching at universities in America, China, Hong Kong, Japan, and Singapore, I made careful observation of families and youngsters, and found commonalities and differences. While children are loved around the world, their upbringing can vary enormously by societies and families. One key difference that stands out between American and East Asian parents, kin, and teachers is the greater emphasis of Asians on their children's conduct and future than in the U.S. While Americans treat childhood, and often adolescence, in large part as a carefree time when physical growth and having fun take precedence over mental development, Asian children are disciplined to arduous study and advance from the lowest grades to higher education through many gate-keeping examinations. Americans and Asians should reflect on that contrast and see if some middle ground might be feasible.

The springtime of life should be a precious, enjoyable time for every child. The leading premise of this book is that children's early life experiences forever shape their ability to learn, think, and conduct their adult lives. Learning should proceed from infancy through youth with no sacrifice of youthful joys and potentials. Fulfilling both children's young and future lives can be exciting and rewarding for them and their caregivers.

During my professional career I published many academic articles, monographs and books that required pedantic footnotes and citations. I wrote this book for general readers who do not crave the scholarly style. However, I have provided adequate background information in the Index and Notes section at the end, which provides information of individuals, groups, and sources cited in the text.

CHAPTER ONE

CHILDREN'S FUTURES BEGIN AT BIRTH

> And they brought unto him also infants, that he would touch them: but when his disciples saw it, they rebuked them. But Jesus called them unto him, and said, Suffer little children to come unto me, and forbid them not: for of such is the kingdom of God. Verily I say unto you, Whosoever shall not receive the kingdom of God as a little child shall in no wise enter therein.
>
> Luke 18:15–17 (KJB)

Welcoming little children unto him, Jesus blessed them for their newborn purity and goodness, and said that adults should be likewise wholesome and worthy. This book follows his wisdom, as it discusses the proper and improper raising and teaching of children for their futures. To start, let's consider six questions:

1) When do children begin to think and learn?

2) What period of life is most critical to a person's future?

3) Who are most important in children's education: teachers or parents?

4)   What are the most crucial factors in parenting and teaching?

5)   What is the proper way to raise and teach children?

6)   Is America's educational system one of the best in the world?

Answers arise as we go from infancy to family, school, and the nation.

Early Language Acquisition and More Are Time-Framed

It may be surprising to think of little, helpless babies as recording and decoding processers, but they are born ready and keen to grasp language. Babies absorb rudiments of whatever language surrounds them, and their brains work hard to make sense of it all with born facilities for just that purpose. About this phenomenon, Dr. Christopher A. Thurber, clinical psychologist and author of *The Summer Camp Handbook*, wrote, "Children learn language not by rote, but by a seemingly effortless interaction between their sponge-like brains and their language-rich environments." Whether parents think it is always commendable or not, the vocabulary of teenagers reflects the same facility of absorbing language. Shakespeare, the superb observer of human life, has young Juliet declaring that although she had only heard Romeo speak one hundred words before, she recognizes his voice as soon as he says a word.

Born with the ability to start discriminating phonemes in the language spoken near them, babies learn about fifty by their sixth month. Phonemes are the smallest language sounds that carry meaning, such as discriminating between the initial sounds of *lip* and *rip* and *big* and *pig*. Called "mouth moves," phonemes indicate possible word meaning. As kids learn to spell, they connect phonemes to graphemes (shapes of alphabetic letters). We confronted the phoneme phenomenon with my granddaughter, who was adopted from China when the girl was a year and half. When she did not speak for very long, I realized that her phoneme recognition remained geared to the language spoken by her Chinese caregivers before her adoption. Gradually picking up American phonemes from her family's speech, the girl chatters away now and enjoys playing word games. Although infants are small and children are immature, their brains are working overtime to grasp and sort out meaning. What kids hear and see what their parents and others say and do affect them. Hearing my young son voice profanity in Chinese with perfect accent and articulation that I had uttered only once or twice when upset, I never repeated my error again and told him that Dad had misspoken and apologized.

A child's first three years are crucial for language acquisition, when babies pick up basics of any language spoken around them, even the most difficult. The in-born mechanism that helps them is known to psychologists as the Language Acquisition Device (LAD), which was first identified by Noam Chomsky of Harvard, who described LAD as the "infinite use of finite means." If kids go six years after birth with little or no human language spoken with and near them, they never learn to speak properly, as happened to children captured and reared by wild animals in Europe. Rescued after the age of six, they growled like the Bear-girl of Fraumark, who was found living with bears in 1767 when she was eighteen, and barked like the Wolf-child of Sekandra in 1872, who was recovered at age six. In connection with the then popular movie, *Dances With Wolves*, the *Daily Star* newspaper of Bangladesh reported on April 17, 1991:

> A tragic orphan brought up by a pack of wild wolves will never be able to live like a normal man, say doctors. The boy who *really* danced with the wolves was aged about seven when he was found twenty-nine years ago in the wastes of Southern Russia by a team of oil explorers. He howled like a wolf and savagely bit one of the oilmen, who christened him Djuma—the Wolf Boy. Professor Rufat Kazirbayev said doctors had battled to reeducate him to act like a normal human being, but failed. They are now giving up the fight. Professor Kazirbayev said that, "His mind is with the wolves. He will howl at the moon for the rest of his life.

There have also been revolting cases over the years when families isolated and hid children, particularly illegitimates, in attics and basements after their birth. Although the secluded children were fed and cleansed, parental speech and tenderness were nil. When others uncovered the abuse after the children passed six, it was too late; like the animal children they too never learned to speak normally. Their tragedy clearly demonstrates that children must be nurtured with much more than nourishment. As this book proceeds, the reader will learn how varying differences in how kids are raised and taught affect their development and life potentials.

In October 2009, researchers at UCLA, UC-Berkeley, and the University of Pittsburgh announced results of a national study of eight thousand Latino children that helps to explain why so many children of poor and immigrant Latino families lag behind white middle-class children in vocabulary, listening, and problem-solving skills. They found that Latino babies are generally healthy with lower mortality rates, and their mothers smoke and drink less than white and black women. However, although the cognitive (thinking, reasoning and memory) level of poor Latino babies nine- to fifteen-months-old equaled that of same-aged non-Latino infants, when the same Latino children were two- to three-years-old, their cognitive level compared poorly, with deficient word comprehension, use of whole sentences, and assembling puzzles. Professor Bruce Fuller of UC-Berkeley, coauthor of the report, said, "Cognitive skills and language during toddler years are a strong predictor of who will do well in kindergarten and early elementary grades." According to the researchers, the poor cognitive and language handicaps of Latino children stem from the low educational level of their Latino mothers. The mothers admitted that they do not try to teach their children, because they believe that is the role of the schools. Besides early learning programs for young children, such as Head Start and Early Head Start, such mothers must be taught to overcome their neglect of their young children's cognitive development. Budding parent training programs attempt to fill that gap, such as the Abriendo Puertas of Families in Schools in Los Angeles

County. As philosopher George Santayana said, "A child educated only at school is an uneducated child."

Computers' intricate operating systems and software mimic our brain's need for language to reason, learn, remember, and communicate. Faulty programming of a PC means that it won't function, and users' poor knowledge and use of PC formats and language will not get them very far. Our brains must be properly programmed to function; how well depends on childhood exposure to and training in language. Those who want their kids to learn more than one language should refer to bilingualism in the Index and Notes section at the end of this book.

In recent years many researchers and groups have tied childhood development to adulthood outcomes as I've also done for years. The National Scientific Council on the Developing Child has concluded that children's early life experiences *forever shape* their ability to learn, think, and conduct their adult lives, as stated in this book's introduction. Studying the personalities of 144 diverse individuals aged past 50, a research team led by Christopher Nave found strong similarity to what their elementary teachers had described in their personality ratings of the individuals as young kids. That means that personality characteristics form early and stay the same through life.

Many economists contend that improvements in early education would advance America's future prosperity. Nobel laureate economist at the University of Chicago James Heckman and coauthor Flavio Cunha wrote, "Childhood is a multistate process where early investments feed into later investments. Skill begets skill; learning begets learning." Their studies found that sustained attention and assistance to disadvantaged kids from early childhood through their teens brought about dramatic results in social skills and school achievement. Rob Grunewald and Arthur J. Rolnick of the Federal Reserve Bank of Minneapolis also concluded that boosting public support for early childhood education would provide "extraordinary returns compared with (other) investments in the public, and even private, sector." Also calling for more investments on children, Angel Gurria, Secretary-General of the Organisation for Economic Co-operation and Development (OECD), said in a 2009 speech that it was a crisis that nations, such as the U.S., do not adequately finance and attend to the education and health of young children. However, before any of these ambitious plans can be implemented to promote youths' future effectiveness as adults, major reforms in America's educational system must come first, as chapter six discusses, such as revolutionary improvements in teacher education and curricular strategy and standards, such as the Common Core State Standards proposes.

Why are mental developments during childhood so important to children's futures? Besides language learning, a child's capacity to think and learn and perform multitudinous tasks in later life begins with the growth and buildup of neurons (gray matter) in the brain and the mental processes they serve. Neurons and their interconnections are the brain's workhorses. As the brain produces neurons on a need basis, children who have loving, interactive parents and teachers develop brains richly interwoven with neurons, unlike kids that are treated negligently.

Dr. Judith Rapoport of the U.S. National Institute of Mental Health reported a seventeen-year study in 2006 that found that the brains of highly intelligent children

develop differently from the brains of children with average intelligence. She and associates concentrated on the
cortex, the thin sheet of neurons around the outer surface
of the brain where higher mental functions are processed.
They discovered that while average children (IQ scores
of eighty-three to 108) reached peak cortex growth at
age seven to eight, very bright youths (IQ scores of 121 to
149) reached their peak cortex thickness about age thirteen, with greater dynamic pruning of redundant neuron
connections to make way for new neurons. According to
Rapoport, because brains of high IQ youths are plastic, it
promotes the "sculpturing or fine tuning of parts of the
cortex, which support higher-level thought."

I pause to forewarn caregivers of the harm that kids
can suffer if their heads are struck hard; this is especially
so when babies' craniums haven't hardened, and the tops
of their heads are still soft with cartilage. It's good that
there are fewer cartoons on TV today, such as *Popeye* and
The Three Stooges, which portrayed head blows and falling
down as comedy. In 2009, the National Football League
began serious study of football players' concussions to set
up stronger safeguard rules, such as tougher penalties for
trauma-producing tackles and greater caution when players suffer concussions. Helmets alone cannot protect players from life-shortening brain damage that is only detect-
able by autopsy after death. NFL retirees fifty years and
older suffer dementia at the rate of six times greater than
non-players.

Besides cognitive abilities, socio-emotional characteristics also develop early. Studies of rats by Dr. Moshe Szyf
of McGill University have found that pups that have been
unsparingly licked and groomed by their mothers grow to

be less fearful and better adjusted than pups whose mothers were inattentive. He also found that daughter rats go on to treat their own babies as their mothers had handled them. Extending his research from rats to humans, Szyf found that poor childrearing influenced proclivity to suicide. Nurture affecting nature, beneficial genes are triggered or hampered by how rat pups and children are cared for. Since many of the suicide cases Szyf studied had involved childhood abuse, he inferred that mood controls in the brain's hippocampus had been switched off to become "frozen assets." If genes that affect behavior can be turned on or off by the way children are raised, it is possible that teachers also induce or inhibit genes. Rapoport's findings with neurons infer the likelihood that the cortex of high IQ children continues to grow into their middle school years.

The Philosophical Baby, written by Alison Gopnik, a cognitive psychologist at the University of California-Berkeley, provides insights into young children's minds. Not only does she accord with the above researchers that babies are actively thinking and struggling to understand, their early experiences are developmental to their future. Gopnik wrote that "Children's brains construct a kind of unconscious causal map, an accurate picture of the way the world works" (page 39), as in imitation. For example, her discussion of how children relate to their parents' reports of their childhoods sheds light on this book's emphases on attachment and the authoritative-engaging style of managing children. She said that parents who recounted unhappy relations with their parents "in a thoughtful, organized way" (making "a coherent causal picture") were likely to have securely attached kids. Parents who told their children that they had unhappy childhoods with their parents but could not recall and tell much "were less likely to have secure children" (page 188).

Dr. Maria Montessori, the distinguished child-centered educator, believed that what young children absorb from their parents and surroundings shapes their minds, characters, and personalities. Therefore, according to Montessori, "order, beauty, harmony, symmetry, love, joy, and peace (must) surround the child," and that there is no exposure to "violence, profanity, discord or parental argumentation." William Wordsworth's poem (1802), "My Heart Leaps Up When I Behold," has the following prophetic line: "The Child is father of the Man," or in today's parlance, "The Child is the parent of the Adult."

Inhibiting Forces

Although everyone would strongly agree that doing a good job in raising and teaching children promotes their growth and future prospects, reality for many kids contradicts that avowal, as shown for the poor Latino children. It's unfortunate that there are so many parents and teachers who are pathetic caregivers. There is certainly much to do and handle at home and in the classroom, but consider these questions: "Is there a consistent, meaningful strategy in what happens day after day?" If critical daily moments at home and the classroom were recorded on camera, would they be a source of caregivers' pride or regret? Am I really trying to improve? For example, many parents and teachers place strict rules on children and hotly demand that they be obeyed, but in actual practice, the strictures are overlooked. Are Sunday values contradicted and forgotten the rest of the week? Wishy-washy, erratic parenting and teaching is often seen in treating favorites differently from other children. When parents, relatives, and teachers mistreat children through neglect and malicious outbursts and actions, ameliorating redress and reform are rare. As Jackie Kennedy Onassis said, "If you bungle raising your children, I don't think whatever else you do well matters very much."

Later, when styles of managing children are discussed, authoritative-engaging parents and teachers will be shown to have their act together. While we accept no leeway in the professional competence of physicians and pilots, diversity is tolerated in the dedication and ability of parents and teachers. After passenger pilots are trained and certified, their skills are often reviewed. When pilots violate FAA regulations, they can lose their license to fly, which happened in 2009 when pilots overflew their destination by 150 miles as they attended to their personal laptops instead of the flight. After teachers are certified and tenured, their teaching ability is rarely reassessed. Why is teaching quality variable? Why are U.S. teachers' salaries far lower than that of airline pilots and other professionals? The answer lies mainly with the relative ease to become a teacher, compared to the rigorous selection, training, certification, and review of pilots and other professionals. Despite superior teachers that can be found, there is much to improve in our teaching profession and educational system, as chapter six examines.

As for parents, the reality is that many vary in how much they actually love, desire, and do for their offspring. Giving birth does not automatically produce loving and capable parents. On this, Michael Levine said, "Having children makes you no more a parent than having a piano

makes you a pianist." Humans are still biologically engi-
neered to reproduce as in primitive times when life was
short and dangerous. Sex is such a powerful instinct; the
magnitude of its gratification is as antiquated as our use-
less appendix. Any proposals for laws that would regulate
childbearing would be condemned as sacrilege, which is
clear from the volatile controversies over sex education
and abortion. Since the unrestricted freedom to bear children is here to stay, parents must be urged and helped to
do what is right for their kids. While begetting children is
simple, raising and educating youths well must be stressed
as a commandment. As candidate Barack Obama said at a
Chicago on Father's Day 2008, "Any fool can have a child.
It's the courage to raise the child that makes you a father."
Let's rephrase the last sentence to say, as now President
Obama would agree with: It's the love, knowledge, and
dedicated commitment to properly raise children that
makes you a true parent. He repeated his urging Father's
Day 2010.

Love and dedication are vital but insufficient by themselves to raise a child properly, for knowledge and wisdom
are also required. Since many parents do not always seek
reliable information, they often fall prey to word-of-mouth
notions, as if they were scientifically proven. Two examples
make the point. A popular canard that circulated is that
playing music composed by Wolfgang Amadeus Mozart
during pregnancy and for infants boosted children's intelligence. It stemmed from a 1993 study in *Nature* that reported
college students had a slight, temporary IQ gain in tasks
while listening to a Mozart sonata. Those results have never
been replicated. Yet, distortions of the original study spread
like wildfire to include infants and even the unborn. The

respected journal, *Pedicatrics,* reported in March 2010 that one in five parents still believe that vaccines cause autism and hesitate to vaccinate their children, even though the 1998 study claiming that vaccinations cause autism had been found to be flawed.

Prisons are overloaded with those who were disadvantaged by miserable childhoods. A troubling report by the National Center on Family and Homelessness said that one in fifty U.S. children, a total of 1.35 million, lived with their homeless families in 2005–06. Texas, California, and Louisiana led the country in having the highest percentages of kids in shelters, motels, autos, and on the streets. Children are big losers as they confront deprivation, violence, and rape. According to Stand Up for Kids and government reports, there are about 1.6 million homeless youths who are on their own—runaways or kicked out of their homes annually, most returning within a week. Combining the numbers for those homeless with families and out on their own means that nearly three million children are living in downtrodden conditions. This does not count poor children living with families in their own domiciles. Founded by Richard L. Koca, Stand Up for Kids finds and aids street youths twenty-one years and younger. On October 26, 2009, the *New York Times* published a lengthy report titled "Recession Drives Surge in Youth Runaways," which said,

> Over the past two years, government officials and experts have seen an increasing number of children leave home for life on the streets, including many under thirteen. Foreclosures, layoffs, rising food and fuel prices, and inadequate supplies of low-cost housing have stretched families to the extreme, and

those pressures have trickled down to teenagers and preteens.

Pertinent to chapter three's discussion of how authoritarians mismanage children, many of the desolate youngsters covered in the NYT's report ran away to escape their abusive parents.

Attachment and Social Interaction

Superior parents and teachers manifest positive attachment and social interaction, which are discussed here and in other chapters. The proper nurturance of children by parents and teachers induces attachment trust and security from which awareness, learning readiness, and good spirits spring and grow. Parallels can be found in all social ties, as columnist Roger Cohen (*New York Times*, May 26, 2008) so ably described as MAC (Mutually Assured Connectivity), in contrast to MAD (Mutually Assured Divide). Parents' MAC attachment with children, who are usually their own flesh and blood, can come naturally through devoted, unselfish commitment.

Teachers must establish MAC rapport with students that relates with but differs from the attachment and social interaction between parents and children. Minus parents' bosom affection and diverse household activities, teacher-student relations also involve far more individuals than in families. Surpassing the humdrum routine of ordinary classrooms with strategic and tactical know-how and planning, superior teachers infuse inspiration and wisdom through their positive rapport with learners, often more influential than parents. For example, Jesus and his disciples, Socrates who mentored Plato, Plato who taught Aristotle, and President James A. Garfield, who lauded Mark Hopkins, his Dartmouth College teacher, when he said on December 28, 1871: "I am not willing that this discussion should close without mention of the value of a true teacher. Give me a log hut, with only a simple bench, Mark Hopkins on one end and I on the other, and you may have all the buildings, apparatus, and libraries without him." Many teachers suffer regret more than relief as I did when school years ended, along with their student attachments. With old class photos in hand, I look nostalgically at the young faces and wonder how the kids, now grown-ups probably with children of their own, are doing. Let me paraphrase an apt quote from The Talmund: "When you teach your children, you teach your children's children."

Let's understand what social interaction is

At the core of true friendship and love, warm, positive social interaction produces bonding attachment (MAC) between individuals that induces their desire to connect and relate with each other. Social psychologists found in WWII research that it made all the difference in whether unit morale and cohesiveness were good or poor. On the other hand, producing fear, anxiety, and resistance, negative social interaction (MAD) is found when people are confined with those they want to avoid, but cannot escape, such as having bosses who mismanage workers. Because young children are so heavily dependent on their parents and teachers, what they experience at home and school is extremely critical to their development.

Following up on John Bowlby's development of attachment theory as many others have, Jeffry Simpson,

social psychologist at the University of Minnesota, studies
the effect of early interpersonal relationships on people's
later lives. He found that if a child's attachment and social
interaction with parents are insecure and aversive at age
one, he or she is likely to have negative interpersonal relationships at age twenty-one and on. Therefore, poor parent-child relations can produce insecure kids who become
school underachievers, and adults who are poor lovers and
parents and insecure with people in general. Poor rapport
with teachers reinforces the negative.

Sending me reprints of their research studies on mothers, which I believe also apply to teachers, Elizabeth Meins
and her psychology colleagues at Britain's University of
Durham have found telling differences in how mothers
handle attachment and social interaction. Comparing
high and low quality mother-child relations, she reported
that "mothers who scored high on sensitivity (show) more
acceptance, cooperation, and accessibility in their inter-
actions with their infants." Mothers with high maternal
sensitivity get to understand their babies so well that they
are able to anticipate and promptly respond to their wants
and needs. Besides handling their babies' physical needs,
such as feeding and changing diapers, high sensitivity
mothers also treat babies as thinking beings, a highly significant point. As they interact with their infants, high
sensitivity moms constantly pour out abundant parentese (baby talk). Dr. Meins said that mothers of securely
attached children use interactive tutoring methods that
elicit back-and-forth response, and they describe their
toddlers in terms of their mental growth. Meins found
that well-attached children mature earlier in language and
play skills than children of low-minding mothers.

Recent studies of classrooms and teachers by University of Virginia (UV) researchers, involving Dean Robert C. Pianta, appear to reinforce the importance of positive social interaction and attachment. However, the UV teams do not use those and other psychological terms. Seeking explanation from them for months and asking if they were aware of my book, *Social Interaction in Educational Settings*, the dean finally emailed me, "we use everyday terminology so that educators can more easily understand our work and interpret the findings." More on this under Pianta in the Index and Notes. Sampling 2,400 four-year-olds in 671 pre-K classrooms, they found that children's academic and language skills flourished when they received "greater instructional support, such as feedback on their ideas and encouragement to think in more complex ways...when teachers showed more positive emotions and were sensitive to children's needs." Also, such teachers were able to modify the problems of misbehaving children. Since results of the pre-K study by the University of Virginia researchers matched results of their earlier research on first-graders, there is reason to believe that the same teaching qualities would be effective at later grades.

It's very important to note that the UV researchers found that many criteria the National Institute for Early Education Research (NIEER) uses to evaluate school quality, such as class size, curricula, and teachers' education, made no difference in children's achievement. They found that teaching quality varied "tremendously" within the same schools or preschool centers, even when NIEER criteria were satisfied. Therefore, evaluating the quality of schools is not the same as evaluating teachers, since a school rated as acceptable or even outstanding can have poor teachers. This means parents should decide where to send their kids, not so much by selecting the "right" school, but looking for the best individual teacher. The best teachers maximize children's learning, no matter their years of college and the adequacy of the schools' facilities. Teacher education and certification must focus on what truly produces teaching effectiveness, and do so to the point of rewarding teacher candidates who can develop skillful social interaction and MAC attachment with youngsters and eliminating those who cannot learn to do so.

Dean of the UV Curry School of Education, Dr. Pianta said that state oversight and in-service training were important, but the "toughest to get right." He added that requiring teachers to complete so many hours of in-service training would not be useful if the training was not focused on how well teachers connect with (social interaction) students. In 2009, Pianta and Megan W. Stulman found from their extensive study of 820 first-grade classrooms in seven hundred public, charter, and private schools across thirty-two states that only 23 percent of the classrooms could be judged to be of "high quality" in social and emotional climate and teaching practices. They said that first-grade classrooms in private schools were "less likely to be in the highest-quality groups" than those in public schools. Since first-grade teachers are the first to systematically teach reading to children and stimulate their learning, they are esteemed by educators. My daughter, who is now a surgeon, had such a competent, warmhearted first-grade teacher that the girl grew out of her shyness and became an apt learner. Our society should adequately reward such outstanding teachers and recognize their vital importance.

Psychologists have long believed that infants develop poorly if they are raised without tender care and loving intimacy. I recall from my studies that psychology textbooks covered this issue with photos of institutionalized children looking lost and forlorn. Nevertheless, institutions for abandoned babies and abused children have continued to function with limited staff and poor funding support. Refusing research access to psychologists for long, authorities prevented them from ascertaining if institutionalized children faced life-threatening problems.

At last, scientific confirmation of what the lack of attachment and poor, restrained social interaction produce was documented in 2007. With funds from the John D. and Catherine T. MacArthur Foundation and Richard David Scott Endowment, U.S. researchers, led by Dr. Charles A. Nelson III, worked with counterparts in Bucharest, Romania, who had access to that city's six institutions for abandoned children (Alas, so many!). Nelson's team reported results for infants forty-two- to fifty-four-months-old in three environments: (1) normal families with parents, (2) foster homes, and (3) orphanage institutions. Infants living with their parents (1) had IQ scores with normal averages of just over one hundred. Babies who went to foster homes soon after brief stays at orphanages (2) scored above eighty, but lower than (1). IQ scores of institutionalized babies (3) were the lowest, in the seventies. Intelligence tests typically rate those who score lower than eighty as mentally retarded. There is no mistaking the results of the orphanage study—babies must have loving care and intimacy, which come from positive social interaction and MAC attachment. If they are lacking, children's mental development and potentials are diminished years before they go to school.

What I mean about fulfilling potentials is what humans can become in their lives through development of what they possess at birth, their mental and physical being. University education is increasingly vital, not just for degrees and certificates and greater job options and earnings, but for studies that can enlarge mental power and awareness. It is disturbing that many students entering college today require remedial courses in math and reading, which faults their previous twelve years of education. Youth in the dawn of what a person becomes is like Jesus Christ's parable of sowing seed on "the way side," "stony places," "thorns," or "good ground" (Matthew 13:1–9, KJB). Using that veritable lesson, I liken babies that are born blank and innocent with a lifetime before them to seed and how they are raised and taught, whether through positive or negative child rearing and education.

Living in Montana, I enjoy its climate's evolution through the seasons–each day, week, and month passing into the next. Spring's budding traces gradually dismiss winter's cold to forecast summer's warmth and flourish and in turn autumn's lovely colors. As I work in my gardens and lawns, the Chinese philosophy of Daoism often come to mind, for it stresses change and the harmony of universal nature, each element affecting others in intricate unity. For example, the earth's rotation around the sun produces night and day and the seasons. From life experiences, we know heat from cold and learn to appreciate happiness by experiencing sadness and the joy of homecoming against loneliness. When I plant seeds and tend to their growth with patient care, in time my vegetables and flowers bear fruit, i.e. cause and effect blended together. Coupling Daoism with Christ's parable of sowing seed on favorable or poor ground, we should realize that the environment and each day, week, month, and year of raising and teaching the young can effect progress or decline.

The words, "Time wastes too fast...," were handcopied from Laurence Sterne's novel, *Tristam Shandy*, by Thomas Jefferson's beloved wife, Martha, before she died in 1782 at the age of only 34. Human lifetimes are brief; from birth to age twenty consumes a quarter of one's life. Forging a career to about forty means the average person's life is half spent. Descendant of revolutionary greats, Henry Adams wrote, "A teacher affects eternity; he can never tell where his influence stops." Applying his famous line to parents, as well as teachers, we get a powerful sense of their joint responsibility for the future lives of children. Many who have been inspired by that quote do not realize that what Adams meant was that teacher effects could be either positive or negative. His futurist point on affecting "eternity" should be taken to heart.

The following adds a colorful dimension to the above by describing what this author experienced as a youngster.

Negative and Positive Social Interaction in My Youth

Thanks to Presidents JFK and LBJ and their congresses, my children had the benefits of the 1964 civil right law curtailing discrimination and racism, which I had experienced as a youth. President Harry Truman's order to desegregate the military meant that I served in an integrated Army where I never faced racism. Before those revolutionary changes, overt racism was often blatant in supposedly Christian America. During World War II on the main street of my California hometown, grown men would haul me up by the collar and belt and shriek in my face. "Are you a Jap?" Struggling to get free, I shouted, "So what, you big bully! Why aren't you in uniform like all my uncles?" Also reflecting the racist tone of those times throughout the nation, not one passerby admonished the bullies for abusing a boy. In desperation, my mother pinned a big button on my shirt, which said, "I am Chinese-American, not the enemy." The button was soon lost, no doubt a collector's item today. Disowning my Japanese-American pals, who had been unjustly locked up with their families in internment camps, would have been betrayal to our friendship.

Shaking me by the shoulders and spouting racist slurs, my sixth-grade teacher used me as a scapegoat when she was at her worst. The chief thing learned that semester was how to read her moods. Assigned a seat by her desk where she often grabbed me in a flash and shook me until my glasses fell to the floor for nothing I had done, I studied the big woman's face with intensity. Her bulbous nose became my warning signal, for powdered up in the morning, she was relatively mild. Yet, as the day wore on and her demonic rage mounted, with fearful fascination I saw the powder abate as the pores on her big nose seeped rings of oil that eventually merged to blare *red alert*.

Lining up the girls on one side of the room and the boys on the opposite side, the teacher rapid-fired multistage arithmetic problems to see who could solve them first. Since only one of us boys would ever volunteer, the girls would always win. At times she called on one pupil to answer and trashed boys who gave the wrong answer or did not respond, but was mild with erring girls. So, besides her racism, the teacher disliked boys. Since age twelve, hearing numbers has been cramped by a mental block of rejection, even taking phone numbers, unless spoken slowly. Whether through war exigencies and signal corps training to enunciate clearly, some numbers to be said with the -er suffix, such as niner for nine, I experienced no mental block in the army.

Innocence lost, I learned early on that there are people who are dangerous victims of their inner demons and might be out for me. As many see others only as caricatures and less complex and whole than they are, their fallacies can engender bigotry and hateful malice. Many just didn't give a hoot in those pre-civil rights days. On sight of my brothers and me, the proprietor of an auto paint shop that we passed daily shouted vicious sarcasm punctuated with his spray gun. Throughout my youth, such demons raised my resolve to persevere, but they also enhanced anxiety and doubts concerning my identity. Although my parents commiserated, they never complained at school. They told me to do my best, which meant that people, like my sixth-grade teacher, were problems I had to endure and handle on my own. All of which forced me to be observant and introspective of others; perhaps that's why I became a psychologist. To explain why my parents did not protest my sixth-grade teacher and others for their bigotry, it was taboo in those days for nonwhites to confront institutions and abusers, especially to dispute racism. Illustrative of those contradictory times, my fourth and fifth-grade classes were at a school named after Luther Burbank, the horticulturist who perfected the potato but served as the secretary of the local anti-Chinese association that was committed to racial hatred.

Fortunately, I encountered good people in my hometown of Santa Rosa, CA who gave me perspective to distinguish good from bad and right from wrong. I shall never forget the MAC love and warmth of the Congregational Church congregation and Rev. Gordon Foster and Rev. Withington before him. When the Presbyterian pastor became an Army chaplain, Rev. Foster assumed the herculean task of ministering both churches. Only a year since my nearsightedness had been discovered and my reading ability lagged, competent, good-hearted Miss Roman, my fifth-grade teacher, leaned over me and said she would help if I wanted to learn to read. One thing she did was to make me the star of a play, in which I had to learn to read long paragraphs pasted on the back of a big, cardboard bear. As I read the long dialogue, Miss Roman had me flipping both arms of the hero bear that she attached to thread spools. During the trauma in sixth grade, I could recall compassionate Miss Roman.

Squeezed among the stores and banks circling my hometown's old courthouse stood a newsstand with comic books. Tired of catching us sneaking reads, the owner let my brother and me read the comics—Terry & the Pirates, Buck Rogers, and Dick Tracy, the favorites—with the proviso that we preserve the books' new-look quality and read them on a stool he set up for us. Thanks to his zenith act, my reading competence accelerated and I moved on to the wonders of books at the library, the first being Daniel Defoe's *Robinson Crusoe*. The man's kind favor was like the beer joint owner in Greenville, Florida, who

let a blind boy play the jukebox and then the piano,—
not that I approximated the fame of the great musician,
Ray Charles. Gestures of humanity do make for a better
world. There are many good people like that and unfortunately many who aren't. Let's "accent the positive and
negate the negative," by realizing that instilling hate and
bigotry into the raising and teaching of children seriously
harms everyone and the society, as it is akin to poisoning
the well of human nature. Americans should take pride in
the heartwarming stories of NFL players, Scott Fujita and
Michael Oher, and their loving families.

Researching why the Chinese and other Asians have
been maligned by racial prejudice for my book, *Yeee-Hah!*,
I found that racism towards Asians, mostly in western
states, had been largely perpetuated by myths and fears
spewed by self-serving politicians, hack writers, and hard-
luck whites. I have also published academic works on racism that revealed its complex nature, such as how it has
even been perpetuated through chicanery and falsehood
in my discipline of psychology–"Addressing psychology's
problems with race." It's gratifying that racism and other
forms of discrimination have faded in the U.S. through
the civil rights laws and the proper nurturing of children
by growing numbers of thoughtful parents and teachers.

CHAPTER TWO

THE AUTHORITATIVE-ENGAGING STYLE OF MANAGING CHILDREN

> Your children are not your children./ They are the sons and daughters of Life's longing for itself./ They come through you but not from you,/ And though they are with you, yet they belong not to you... You are the bows from which your children as living arrows are sent forth.
>
> —Kahlil Gibran, "On Children,"
> *The Prophet,* 1923

Following the pioneering research of Dr. Diana Baumrind, developmental psychologists have given much study to parental styles of raising children to better understand human behavior and how it's formed. Their findings with parents can be generalized to teachers as well. Four contrasting styles of managing (raising, teaching, and disciplining) young people have been identified: Neglectful, Authoritarian, Indulgent, and Authoritative. Each has very different consequences for young people's lives. The first three styles that psychologists spurn are analyzed in the next chapter. My adding a second modifying label to their titles, neglectful-indifferent parents give little if any attention to their children, authoritarian-dictatorial parents are autocratic, and indulgent-permissive parents allow their children to freely express themselves and pursue whatever they desire. Discussed in this chapter, the managing style psychologists praise and recommend is authoritative, to which I have added "engaging" to its label.

How children are controlled is important to keep in mind as different styles are discussed, for control involves the use or absence of authority, discipline, guidance, management, oversight, and regulation. How it's managed makes all the difference between the four styles of parenting and teaching. For neglecting-indifferent parents and teachers, control is the laissez-faire denial of duty and responsibility; doing little or nothing with and for children. Authoritarian-dictatorial control is top-down command stressing obedience with little tolerance for flexibility in children's conduct and thought. Indulgent-permissive control is caregivers' appeasement and lenience in what children do and think as they attend to their kids. More challenging of parents and teachers than the other styles, authoritative-engaging control is an ongoing interactive process to promote children's maturing, self-regulating behavior and reasoning.

The authoritative-engaging managing style is a balanced approach to raise, teach, and discipline children. Authoritative-engaging parents and teachers believe that youths should be raised and taught to become thoughtful, self-sufficient people. To fulfill that aim, they and their kids actively engage in MAC-powered attachment and social interaction. Countering the belief of indulgent-permissive types that children will develop best with minimal control and learn through their self-felt initiatives, authoritative-engaging parents and teachers use their positive attachment to maintain control by explaining and reasoning things out with children. Counseling children to manage themselves and live compatibly with others and their environs, authoritative-engaging parents and teachers want their kids to believe that whatever they do involves their choice, and responsibility as well as that of others. It's not one-sided; simply what indulged kids desire on their own or what dictators demand what must be done. Building on the positive MAC attachment that they formed with infants, authoritative-engaging caregivers gradually extend nurturance to promote their older kids' growing maturity, self-reliance, and self-assessment. Engaging with their youths' needs, actions, and feelings on a strict but fair, one-to-one basis that stresses reasoned balance between control and independence, authoritative-engaging parents and teachers employ extensive verbal social interaction with their youths of a constructive nature.

When their children are mischievous and break rules, authoritative-engaging parents and teachers press them to explain what went wrong, motives, and improvements to follow in the future. Issue-oriented and objective, authoritative-engaging parents want to avoid resentment, shame, and guilt feelings that the authoritarian style imposes on kids. As Dr. Sal Severe, clinical school psychologist in Phoenix advised, "Simply say, other families have their rules, and we have ours. I'm not saying no to make you feel upset. I am saying no because I don't think this is good for you. That's my job—to do what I think is best for you." I would modify the last line by saying, "That's my job—to help you see what's best for you and all of us." As mentioned earlier, abundant dialogue with youngsters bolsters the growth and interconnection of brain neurons and enhances language and intellectual abilities.

Compared to indulgent parents, who dismiss discipline, and dictatorial parents, who order, "Do what I say or else," authoritative-engaging parents say, "Time out. Let's talk this over." Instead of saying, "Put the toys away right now or I'll spank you," engaging parents would say in a collaborative manner, "Shall we put the toys away and get tidy?" Questions dominate what engagers say to children. Children learn to connect actions with consequences, not just for themselves, but also for others. This habitual pattern of cause-effect interaction between grown-up and youngster develops a conscientious mode of MAC, team-member reflection that is lacking with the other styles. It also helps children to be issue-oriented and objective. When kids understand and abide with the standards and expectations of their authoritative-engaging parents and teachers, self-discipline and constructive patterns of behavior take hold.

Telling differences between the indulgent, dictatorial, and engaging styles appear when parents and teachers themselves break rules and are in error. Indulgent types apologize over everything and nothing; dictators are guilty, but blame others; while engagers admit mistakes, saying, "Yes, sorry, I made a boo-boo. It's human to error and I'm human like you. So we learn from our mistakes." While others overstress apologies or admit no faults, authoritative-engaging parents and teachers handle miscues fairly and impartially, as shown by their habitual use of "we" and "us" versus "I" and "you." As writer Mignon McLaughlin wrote, "A parent who has never apologized to his children is a monster. If he's always apologizing, his children are monsters."

In contrast to other managing styles' here-and-now, temporal nature, the authoritative-engaging approach takes a constructive, futuristic perspective. It concentrates on kids' ongoing maturation, with an eye on their tomorrows. Authoritative-engaging parents and teachers often encourage their youths to assess their current progress to think about what they might be like and do in the future, often asking "How're we doing?" Young people are encouraged to study the lives of historic figures to reflect on their shortcomings and accomplishments. Biographies are an excellent approach to understanding human nature and history, as well as demonstrating how childhood relates to adulthood. For example, biographers say that famed World War II General George S. Patton suffered dyslexia, which causes reading and other language problems for about twenty percent of the population. At age twelve, he couldn't read. Supported by loving MAC parents who read to him and using his great ability to memorize, such as whole passages of classics, Patton strived to overcome his handicap and succeeded in regaining admission to West Point after he was sent away for a year. A good example of perseverance, nevertheless, he remained a poor speller all his life. Other famous people have been affected by dyslexia, such as Cher, Einstein, Edison, Woodrow Wilson, and Nelson Rockefeller.

From Luke 2:41–52, (KJB), I can see from their dialogue that Mary and Joseph raised Jesus as authoritative-engaging parents. After searching three days for their son, who they feared had been lost after the family had celebrated the feast of the Passover in Jerusalem, they found him in the temple interacting with priests. Mary said to him, "Son, why hast thou thus dealt with us? Behold, thy father and I have sought thee sorrowing." To which, Jesus replied, "How is it that ye sought me? Wist ye not that I must be about my Father's business?" Following which, Luke wrote, "And they understood not the saying which he spake unto them. And he went down with them and came to Nazareth, and was subject unto them: But his mother kept all these sayings in her heart. And Jesus increased in wisdom and stature, and in favour with God and man."

Childhood and teenage years should be viewed as preparatory stages for life. It follows that authoritative-engaging parents want their youths to be taught at home and school through well-structured instruction that is thoughtful and stimulating. What David Brooks wrote (*New York Times*, March 13, 2009) relates well with this line of thought:

> When he was a boy, his mother would wake him up at 4:30 to tutor him for a few hours before he went off to school. When young Barry complained about getting up so early, his mother responded: "This is no picnic for me either, Buster." That experience was the perfect preparation for reforming American education because it underlines the two traits necessary for academic success: relationships and rigor. The young Obama had a loving relationship with an adult passionate about his future. He also had at least one teacher, his mom, disinclined to put up with any crap.
>
> The reform vision Obama sketched out in his speech flows from that experience. The Obama approach would make it more likely that young

Americans grow up in relationships with teaching adults. It would expand nurse visits to disorganized homes. It would improve early education. It would extend the school year. Most important, it would increase merit pay for good teachers (the ones who develop emotional bonds with students) and dismiss bad teachers (the ones who treat students like cattle to be processed).

We've spent years working on ways to restructure schools, but what matters most is the relationship between one student and one teacher. You ask a kid who has graduated from high school to list the teachers who mattered in his life, and he will reel off names. You ask a kid who dropped out, and he will not even under-stand the question. Relationships like that are beyond his experience.

People who are raised and taught in authoritative-engaging settings are generally self-governing, civil, and responsible. Their social poise and interactive skills are conducive to the well-being of their families and careers. Because attachment bonds continue in time and mature further, engaging parents enjoy enduring relations with their adult children and their families, which they treasure in old age. As Bill Cosby wrote in *Fatherhood*, 1986, "Human beings are the only creatures on earth that allow their children to come back home."

On that note, at an Elderhostel in Berkeley, CA a woman complained to me that her two grown-up sons still lived at home. College graduates, both men worked as waiters at luxurious restaurants. When they accumulate enough cash, they go on far-flung travels together and return home to work again as waiters when their funds are depleted. Telling me that her sons haven't shown any sign of changing their lifestyle, which their father tolerates, the frustrated lady said that she keeps raising their "rent" but to no avail. Their family appears to represent special cases of parental and sibling attachment.

Raising Our Children with the Authoritative-Engaging Style

What follows illustrates how my family used the author-itative-engaging style to raise our children. As many parents do, my wife and I read storybooks to our children as they sat on our laps and at our feet. Preschoolers especially enjoy story readings. Not just rote reading, we interacted with the kids by interjecting questions and accenting points now and then, such as "What's going to happen next?" and stressing certain sentences and pictures, "Let's stop and see if you understand what that means." My wife and the children's mother, Irene, read frequently each day with dramatic feeling and suspense. I can still hear her clamorous reading of *Chicken Little*'s warning cry in high-pitched tone, "The sky is falling!" which always raised a big smile when it penetrated my study. At times, I would join them hilariously flapping my arms like a terrified bird and shouting, "The sky is falling!" As I "flew" around the room, the children vigorously applauded and laughed.

More than mere entertainment and having the kids listening quietly, our book readings included interactive involvement, (pointing to the words) "Now that's just what I read. What's that word and what does it mean? Want to read it yourself?" "Do we want to be good (or bad) like that?" "What do you think will happen next?" Before they could read, we made regular library visits, where they freely chose books to check out. Though they tended at first to select books with attractive pictures, they then sought substance and expressed pride in their choices, "I picked that book." After her fifth birthday, the oldest read or more accurately recited their favorites to her brother, which tickled me when she imitated Irene's and my tone and questions. Weekly library visits became a habit for many years. For the oldest preschooler, I set up her own chair and lamp in a corner of my study, where she sat engrossed in reading for what seemed hours from her pile of storybooks. I instructed her to raise her eyes now and then and look around to relieve and exercise her eyes. Checking her comprehension, I asked for summaries, and she related highlights of favorites and criticized books she regarded as having mediocre stories and/or pictures. A similar reading place for the boy came later.

Their bedtime was 9PM when I laid down with them and told a story with a moral about kids like them that did well or not. When the story ended, we hugged and I bounced them down on their beds after singing:

> Rock-a-bye baby, on the treetop,
> When the wind blows, the cradle will rock,
> When the bough breaks, the cradle will fall,
> And down will come baby, cradle and all.

On June 23, 2010 President Obama relieved General Stanley A. McChrystal from his command of U.S. and NATO forces in Afghanistan. The general's inglorious fall came after a *Rolling Stones* article covered his and his aides' hostile and insubordinate remarks towards many of the nation's top civilian leaders. Checking his daily habits of sleeping only 3–4 hours, running about 14 miles, and eating only one meal, I realized that McChrystal short-changed his wellbeing—if he wasn't physically exhausted he had to be mentally stretched. Psychological research makes it absolutely clear that humans should sleep eight hours each night; some people are OK with a bit less. Sleeping properly each day not only helps to restore one physically, and through deep sleep one reaches what is called the rapid-eye movement (REM) stage when we dream and the mind reviews and sorts out problems and seeks resolution. That's why we often go to bed with problems and awake with solutions. Gen. McChrystal's poor sleep habit helps to account for his arrogant, unguarded behavior. The Army told us GIs in Korea that four hours of sleep a day was sufficient for us to do our job when we could get it; but what about generals, who are the brains behind operations?

Seeing their professor father spending most of his time at home concentrating at his desk and hearing what he and their mother discussed about his academic work had to carry over to the kids. We provided worktables for the youngsters in their carpeted play area where they read, drew, and carried on—an important work center we made much use of. When they were teenagers and we had moved from Wisconsin to California, we purchased a house in which each had their own rooms that were furnished, besides beds, with good study desks, chairs, and lighting. To get the boy a proper chair, which proved to be better than my own, we drove to a far-off furniture sale that was held off of a freight car.

We encouraged our kids to make scrapbooks of their interests, such as panda bears, the favorite animal of the oldest child. Encouraging her interest in pandas and thereby stimulate interest in biology, I brought home panda posters and dolls. Of course, they did more than just scrapbooks. Their favorite playthings were horses mounted on springs that they rocked mightily back and forth. Playing outside one day, they mercilessly attacked bees and amazingly they weren't stung. I told them to stop, saying bees helped people by producing honey. Mumbling "Dumb Daddy!" they rambled away to find something else to do. Soon after, we discussed bees with the help of library books, as that incident, like many others, provided initiative to study and learn. At times, I propped up the oldest before she went to kindergarten with many cushions on a chair next to my desk, where she read as I worked and could study her closely. Locked in my memory box of cherished moments, I can still see her studious demeanor as it reflected her growing learning readiness. Although there were some who said, "She's just a girl. Don't waste your time," I insisted on raising our kids with little differentiation of gender.

Scrapbooks became a prominent activity for the preschoolers.

We provided a large kid-sized table, a big box of crayons, paste, and large sheets of paper that were never exhausted. With children's scissors, they cut pictures and headlines from newspapers and magazines and pasted them into scrapbooks. Many topics, such as the bees and pandas, materialized in scrapbooks or just one-page drawings. When Irene and I found crayon drawings on the wall, they learned that it was a no-no through engaged reasoning and by their helping to clean the mess.

A significant series of scrapbooks dealt with the question people often like to put to youngsters, "What would you like to be and do when you grow up?" When relatives raised the question, we used it to promote discussion about their futures, other people's work lives, and adulthood in general. A number of occupations popped up in our talks on that topic, and I steered the children to consider criteria before making their choices: "You say that you want to be a fireman, but *why* do you want to work as a fireman?" They considered their father's work, but what I did as a professor drew a big blank. Their ignorance on that struck me with humor when my son was overheard explaining my job as a university professor to a neighbor boy, "Oh, he sits at his desk in an office listening to music and he has two phones, really!" At that time, the University of Texas-Austin had an intra-campus phone system besides external lines.

Sporadic discussion on the big question continued for years, sporadically because I wanted projects to emerge from their own choice. Projects would often arise when they had questions about this and that to which I said, "Let's investigate, get answers, and show what we learned." I agree with what psychiatrist Roger A. Lewin said: "Too often we give our children answers to remember rather than problems to solve." I always kept my kids' short attention spans in mind and I wanted them to think on their own. On the lifework project, I suggested that they consider adults they knew and if their occupations might interest them, which brought up jobs they knew nothing about, such as our neighbor, a United Airlines pilot (whose attractive Scandinavian wife went *au naturel* indoors), Uncle Edmund's grocery store, Uncle Edward's engineering job, and Uncle Chester's pharmacy. When their pediatricians came to mind, they thought they had a possible choice of occupation; but I insisted on why. In answer, they mentioned the candy they got from the medics and how nice the MDs were, to which I replied, "Okay, let's draw some pictures of that and let's write captions for them." We could hear the kids talking it over as they worked on their scrapbooks: "We get treats from aunties and other people, so what's so big with doctors?" "Yeah, and I don't like shots!" "But doctors are nice and take good care of us, like when we had the measles."

Importantly, they did more than draw pictures for their scrapbooks. I had them dictate to me what their drawings meant, and I printed their words on a separate sheet. They then copied their statements beneath their drawings. This is a teaching/learning experience that I strongly recommend, as it boosted their writing and reading comprehension. An example of their original efforts is at the end of this chapter.

I sharpened the why question to what their prospective job choices actually did. For one example, the oldest wanted to be a ballerina because of the dancers' lovely dresses she saw on a TV showing of the "Nutcracker Suite." When she curtailed her thumb-sucking, Irene sewed her a lovely ballerina dress as a reward. The boy said that the police and firefighters protect us from harm and bad people, and doctors also help us with checkups and when we get sick and hurt. Picking up on the words, "help us," I asked them to compare how firefighters, police, the milkman, and doctors do good for us and other people. They put aside being milk deliverers, though ours cheerfully put milk bottles straight into the fridge. Since they hadn't encountered any yet, becoming nurses or teachers didn't register for long. An unseen being, they never considered the mail carrier. Having had no direct contact with the police and firefighters, they highlighted their experiences with their pediatricians. After I suggested research to learn more, we searched for library books on ballerinas and dancing, firefighters, police, and medics, as well as exploring the idea of "helping others." Perusing the phone book's yellow pages, they were amazed by the great number of businesses and professions.

Captain Kangaroo was about the only TV program that we allowed them to watch, as it portrayed good manners, respect and fair play for others and to be kind to animals. It amazed me that they paid closer attention to commercials than anything else. Whether Irene or I prompted it or not, they decided that it might be hard to become a doctor because of their serious and helpful work with people's health and ailments. Perhaps the MDs' crowded waiting room, receptionists, and elaborate paraphernalia and polished manner impressed them. I introduced the matter of educational requirements and financial rewards with the example of my situation, similar to medical doctors educationally, but not in subject matter, work, and pay. Over several years when we might go a month or more without focus on the future job issue, they considered more seriously that they would be doctors because they could help others when they were sick and hurt, including their parents and relatives, study and learn, and make a good living. Through high school and college, their MD career ambition strengthened, and both scored as SAT merit scholars. The "self-socialization" theory of Stanford psychologists Eleanor Emmons Maccoby and

Carol Nagy Jacklin helps to explain the course of the children's lifework project. The psychologists concluded that children make inferences that guide their behavior and life goals from the roles and behaviors in which they observe men and women and other boys and girls engage.

When five medical schools accepted the oldest, she decided to go to Yale because its class size of sixty insured a low student-faculty ratio. Today she is a professor of surgery at Ohio State University's College of Medicine, with breast cancer as her research interest. Graduating from high school a year later, our son also sought medical school admission. That aim concluded upon his appointment into the Foreign Service, the elite of federal service and hardest to obtain, since it accepts less than one percent of applicants. Over the years before they entered school, MAC engaging social interaction benefited their mental development and work ethic. Their careers project had some effect, but the greatest outcomes were expanding their curiosity, thinking, and communication and work skills that also grew out of other projects and all we did as a family.

Long-distance social interaction helped my son to end up in the Foreign Service of the U.S. State Department. While teaching at a university in Hong Kong, during a stop at the U.S. Consulate, I spotted a poster announcing the coming of the annual Foreign Service examination. Picking up an application, I saw that the deadline was only several weeks off, and immediately expressed it to Irene in the U.S. with the message to put it in the young man's hands without delay. I added advice that he might want to take the exam for the fun of it and see how he could do. He took the exam and scored well, joining 3,000 out of the 15,000 who had sat for the examination around the U.S., thus beginning further hurdles and FBI checks lasting two years that finally narrowed the 3,000 to about 200 accepted into the service. As this is written, he is serving in Afghanistan as head of the U.S. Provincial Reconstruction Teams, following three years as Consul General in Greece, and many earlier diplomatic tours.

Many of their teachers ranked high as knowledgeable, challenging, and authoritative-engaging educators.

That was not happenstance, for I moved the family, even across the country, in order to enroll the kids in outstanding learning and social environments. Their carefully chosen high school in Southern California, Huntington Beach High School (HBHS), stood out. HBHS' gifted stream offered several honors courses, one being the Model United Nations (MUN) program, which the girl and boy signed up for and was taught by history teacher Lynn Aase. Before we moved from Madison, Wisconsin to Huntington Beach, I had obtained their school records with test results, etc., so that they could be presented in Huntington Beach to ensure their proper class placements.

Based on operations and issues of the United Nations, the MUN program has involved competition between high schools in state, regional, and national MUN simulations. Today, international simulations are also held, and HBHS has sent winning delegations to Russia, France, and Germany. MUN boards assign which nation each school will represent, and the topics that were to be argued in simulations. Like debating contests, impartial judges monitoring the simulations decide which team's presentation wins. Students have to research their assigned country's history, governance, leaders and institutions, and past positions on international issues, such as genocide in Darfur and North Korea's atomic bomb threat. They also had to research rival nations and their competing viewpoints as well as to become familiar with the UN's charter, workings of the Security Council, General Assembly, and the UN's organization and procedures. The format, therefore, involved much research analysis, writing and speaking skills, initiative, and debating prowess. I coached my two to speak clearly and refrain from sniffing and using meaningless interjectors, such as "ah," "and the," and "you know."

Although teams like to represent a permanent member nation in the Security Council that took provocative stances, my children told me that a non-Security Council country that had a big stake in an assigned issue provided opportunity to be outspoken, such as Iran and Israel today. When Huntington Beach's principal secured permission for the MUN students to use resources of the UCLA library, which served as a UN depository, my two youths loaded the family car, which they had nicknamed "The Blue Bomber," with partner students and drove there a number of times on weekends. Pleased with their myriad learning and skills, I complimented how well Mr. Aase handled the course with deft, MAC-type instruction and inspiration.

During the 1977–78 school year, one of HBHS's teams comprised of my two youngsters and a classmate won the state and regional stimulations on the issue of China's one-nation policy and stance toward Taiwan. Advancing to the national simulation held at Harvard University, they won representing the UN delegation of the People's Republic of China. Of course, their debating stance did not mean that they favored the PRC and supported its hard-line on Taiwan. Before the Harvard contest, I had contacted the PRC's UN delegation to inform them of the event and ask if the team might visit them in New York City. It worked out perfectly, as Ambassador Xie and his staff graciously received and congratulated the HBHS team and Mr. Aase. That memorable experience and all that they learned at HBHS through the MUN program and other courses, such as two semesters with an outstanding French teacher, have stood in good stead for our diplomat son and surgeon daughter.

Family Give-and-Take

The above should not give the impression that social interaction in our family always flowed smoothly, without disagreements and problems. Understanding how social interaction operates, if I have made it clear, makes it obvious that what transpired in our kids' development involved give-and-take on major and minor issues and decisions. For a simple example, when my daughter began to apply for admission to medical schools, I urged her to consider six-year MD/ Ph.D. programs that one could enter with only two years of undergraduate studies. Involving students in medicine and research early, MD/ Ph.D. programs help graduates to gain two gate-opening degrees and save costs and time in advancing their careers. In reply to my advice, the girl looked at me sternly with arms akimbo and said, "Dad!" What about the humanities and arts I'd miss if I didn't get a BA degree?" That issue ended right then and there.

Of course we had pets that became valuable members of the household, especially Casey, our intelligent and loving Keeshond dog that came to us as a registered pup and lived fourteen years. We also had a large aquarium with the usual goldfish and guppies. Adding small fish and crawfish from Monona Lake to the aquarium when we lived in Madison, Wisconsin, the kids watched in fascination at how crawdads nipped and almost finished off the original occupants. However, despite my nudges to lend a hand, the children never did much in the pets' care, even after I had showed how Casey learned through operant conditioning to wipe his paws before being let back into the house, thereby wearing out doorstep carpets. Knowing that I enjoyed Casey and the aquarium, they decided that the animals were Dad's responsibility.

We provided our high school youths the use of an auto with gas and maintenance, which the boy drove with the girl and pals as passengers. Besides the oft-repeated talking about safe and careful driving, they knew that they had to be home in time for dinner and then to take turns cleaning up after we dined. Simple to say, but as parents with teenagers realize full well, much social interaction circulated around those and other rules. The youngsters didn't dispute the rules so much as they found excuses to get around them, such as after school sports, messy rooms, and skipping dinner to study for tests. Since dinner was the only time each day when the family gathered and could converse together, Irene and I insisted on our dining policy and their eating properly. Their weekly allowances could be lost for gross violations. I started off the oldest with a dime per week when she entered first grade and the amount was doubled every birthday. I should have started lower, because the girl at 17 got more than my disposable pocket change.

Typical of teenagers, driving and gas consumption raised concerns.

Because teenagers typically feel that they know the ropes and are invulnerable, plus view their parents as cash cows, they can dismiss parental guidance on driving safety and budgeting. The boy and I went round-and-round on auto matters until he had an accident hitting another car by driving too closely, one of many dangers I had forewarned by pointing out driver faults as we rode together. Fortunately, no one was injured. Everything we had interacted about driving hit home. The greatly increased insurance cost to cover his driving dented the family budget, and the shock of his accident caused him to confront the real dangers his sister, himself, and others faced on the road. Because his profound, ameliorating reactions became evident, I hardly said more than, "You have certainly learned a big lesson the hard way," and that he would be without wheels for a month. To this day, he is the most conscientious driver in the family. A well-to-do friend told me that when her teenage son put noisy tail pipes onto the family car, she forbid his driving altogether, which he didn't pick up again until he left home for college. Her severe punishment was counterproductive, since what he learned and endured through his teens became frustration and resentment with no chance to amend his behavior.

My granddaughter is fortunate to have such an understanding and interactive mother. On drives, for example, my oldest interacts with her daughter about the music and talk on the radio and discs, interesting sights being passed, school, piano lessons, etc. A true authoritative-engaging styled parent, my daughter tactfully directs the young girl, such as asking her not to interrupt her conversation with others, for example, "I'm speaking with my daddy right now. You and I can talk later, okay?" My guess is that my children, as perhaps most other youths reared through the authoritative-engaging style, credit their own initiatives and efforts more than their upbringing. If true, other authoritative parents with grown, achieving kids understand my smiling with self-satisfied pride.

What follows is what the oldest wrote and drew when she was five, with answers from her younger brother. I'm sure it stemmed from her looking under my arm as I paused to sip some coffee and her questioning me about the exam I was writing for my students.

This test is about at home. Very good wish No Yes Not Suer

1 Do you play much? yes
2 Do you play recress? no
3 Do you eat much? yes

☆ 100

Drol a line to the opset wird

open ———————— close
up ———————— happy
sad ———————— down
stand ———————— sit
fat ———————— dry
wet ———————— thin

C. 100 ☆

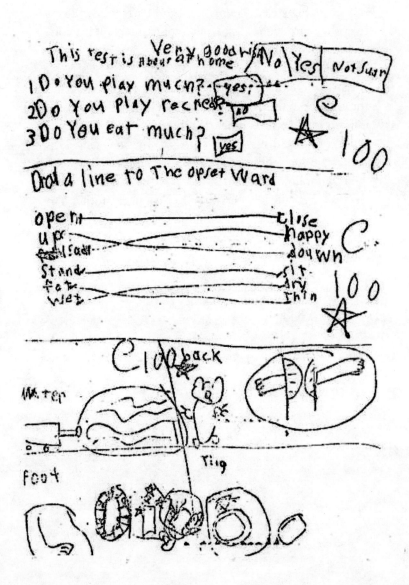

C 100 back

water

foot

Ttig

CHAPTER THREE

CHILD MANAGING STYLES TO AVOID

> Parentage is a very important profession; but no test
> of fitness for it is ever imposed in the interest of the
> children.
>
> —George Bernard Shaw,
> *Everybody's Political What's What* (1944)

Chapter two presented the authoritative-engaging style
of managing children, which developmental psychologists
endorse. This chapter examines three non-recommended
styles to show how they affect the young and their lives,
why they should be avoided, and possible shifts from one
style to another.

The image of American children being raised in
married-couple families is denied by U.S. Census Bureau
reports showing that households are changing signifi-
cantly. Out of the nation's 111.3 million households in
2003, the biggest change from 1970 to 2003 has been a big
drop in married-couple households with their own children—from 40.3 percent to 23.3 percent. One-parent families with children, mostly low-income mothers, increased
to 16.4 percent in 2003 versus 11 percent in 1970. With
America's divorce rate at about 41 percent, many children

live with one parent and may see the other at times, or
live with their grandparents and other kin. As the U.S.
Department of Health and Human Services reported in
2001, 581,000 children were in foster care and go out on
their own when of age. A growing, unknown number of
youths of illegal immigrants live in poverty and suffer ill
health and illiteracy. Adoption Exchange's Web site says,
"Nationwide, 114,000 children wait in state care for adoption. A majority of them are children of minority heritage
who face significant developmental, medical, behavioral,
and/or emotional challenges." These figures show that
numerous children in America live with little or no traditional family associations, and even sense of security.
Facing those social shifts and the challenges they present
to schools, teachers must be well-prepared to manage the
diversity of today's youths.

Since primitive times, the most enduring social group
for humans has been the family. For millennia, families
of men, women, kin, and offspring struggled to survive
through mutual common cause. Moral values, such as the
fifth of the Ten Commandments to honor one's father
and mother, acknowledged the importance of the traditional family. It was not long ago that young women were
expected to marry, bear children, and cohabit in families.
I remember how neighbor friends in Madison, Wisconsin
in the 1970s heatedly pressured their daughter, a dedicated
teacher, to marry and how the young lady maintained her
tight-lipped resistance. My wife and I quietly applauded
her for standing her ground.

Although the capabilities of humans' brains are not
determined by gender, social values traditionally restricted
the life choices of females to marriage, children, and pro-

fessions that accommodate family obligations and working outside the home. Today, women are far less restricted, and more remain single and marry later in life. Those trends should continue as brawn diminishes in importance to brainpower and biases are liberalized. Through millions of years, prehistoric males fulfilled the roles of hunter and warrior, and females served as gatherers of food and guardians of children. Thus, throughout the ages, attractive, well-formed, and amiable women were chosen and protected as mates, which explains how evolution made females better looking and more cheerful than males. In their prime of attractiveness, many young females have yielded to romance and the sex urge. With kids and household duties, their well-being depended on their male breadwinners. One expanding development today is that more women are educating themselves and finding that it is possible to be self-sufficient and, if they choose, also have a family.

Today, personal and social alternatives rival the traditional family. More and more people live alone or unmarried with a companion, and many children are seldom if ever in touch with relatives. When I was a Stanford graduate student in the 1960s, a sociologist said that the only uniform family function remaining in the U.S. was biological; that is, men and women living together and having and raising children. Even that is changing now, as seen in surrogate mothers, substitute pregnancy technologies, same-sex couple families, couples that decide against having children, increasing adoptions of foreign infants, and remarriages that include stepchildren. Surprising and bizarre, paternity DNA studies in Britain have found that about 10 percent of the children in tested families were sired by men other than their fathers. Although the traditional, nuclear family remains the popular image of family, at least in the media, how will increasing social changes, as just related, influence children's happiness and whole-life chances? When there are children, what matters most of all is how they are raised and taught, and why the three management styles this chapter discusses should be avoided.

Schools and teachers cope with increased numbers of troubled youths from impoverished and broken homes, like my Windsor School pupils. Disadvantaged and disoriented youths can be hard to teach and manage, partly because teachers are unprepared to cope with them and may be ill-suited to teach to begin with. Columbine High School–like dangers, youth indigence and deviancy, and increasing numbers of non-English speakers in California and elsewhere in the U.S. have brought about increased challenges for schools. Therefore, managing and disciplining youths who come to school from diverse home environments requires professional skill and know-how.

One sign that the meaning of family has changed in the U.S. is that children born out of wedlock are no longer sneered at as illegitimates, a stigma that such children suffered, but never deserved. Although much change has come about, families in the past were hardly similar and serene. Chapter five's analysis of ten notable persons displays tremendous household and child rearing differences. However, no matter the changes and whatever the settings may be for the young, whether with birth, adoptive or foster parents, grandparents, etc., absolutely nothing differs in the children's need for love, nurturance, guidance, and support for many years as babies, youths, and teenagers.

Raising children is not cheap. Using data it collects from about five thousand households visited and interviewed quarterly, the U.S. Department of Agriculture reported that the cost in 2005 to raise a child from birth to age seventeen for low-income families totaled $182,920; for middle-income (average, $70,500) families, $250,530; and high-income families, a whopping $366,029. For the cost of a child from birth to his or her first birthday, low-, middle-, and high-income families afforded $7,300, $10,220, and $15,190, respectively. For a seventeen-year-old, the one-year cost was $13,790, $18,780, and $27,270, respectively; the higher amount for high-income families was due to costlier education and other expenses, such as travel. Cost-effectiveness per child comes with larger families; infants costing least, with steady percentage increases as the brood grows older. For example, the one-year cost for an average family having three children with a tot aged zero to two, and two teens aged thirteen and sixteen, amounted to $25,030 in 2005, which compares well with the cost for one well-to-do youth above. Reinforcing what this book says about fulfilling children's potentials, the investment costs alone provide reason for parents to do as good a job as possible.

Problems Facing American Families

Chapter one touched on the horrendous cases of children taken by animals, and those secluded with little human contact. That those pathetic youths suffered grievous privations after their rescue from wild animals—never learning to speak—highlights the gravity of meaningful human growth and development during childhood. Chapter five's critical analysis of ten lives demonstrates how different patterns of attachment and rapport with young people can markedly influence their mind-set and behavior as adults.

Caregivers generally report that raising the very young is relatively easy compared to what comes later. As adolescents mature and begin to flap their wings, family relations typically change as youths' self-felt wants and activities take center stage. Although life with teenagers can be challenging and even agitated, families adjust to the fact that peer group norms take precedence over the caregivers' rules and authority. Conforming to rules governing their sleep, dress, study, TV viewing, etc., as young children, many adolescents do about what they want and flaunt traditional norms, which is why many get into trouble. The U.S. Centers for Disease Control and Prevention (CDCP) reported in 2005 that 20 percent of the nation's teenagers use drugs, 25 percent binge drink, and 50 percent are sexually active. In January 2010, using the latest data from the CDCP, the Guttmacher Institute reported that 2006 pregnancy rates among single teenagers rose 3 percent over 2005, with the increase mostly among eighteen- to nineteen-year-old, poor, minority girls. The rate of teen pregnancies had fallen after the seventies and eighties sexual revolution and through 2000–05. Abortions have also decreased.

The CDCP also released results of a national study in 2008 that found that one in four American girls and young women are infected with at least one sexually transmitted disease (STD). About half of the African-American girls aged fourteen to nineteen were infected with at least one of the diseases monitored in the study—human papillomavirus (HPV), chlamydia, genital herpes, and trichomoniasis, a common parasite. That 50 percent figure for blacks compared with 20 percent of white girls. The two most common STD's were HPV (18 percent) and chlamydia (4 percent). Each disease can be serious in its own way. HPV, for example, can cause cancer and genital warts. Fifteen percent had more than one of the diseases. As the *New York Times* (March 12, 2008) reported, "Women may be unaware they are infected ... The infections can also lead to long-term ailments, like infertility and cervical cancer." Dr. Sara Forhan, lead author of the CDCP report, said, "What we found is alarming how fast the STD prevalence appears. Far too many young women are at risk for the serious health effects of untreated STDs."

Checking out HPV, I found Gardasil.com and learned that Merck produces a vaccine to ward off that disease. The Web site said that of the approximately six million new cases of HPV in the United States every year, it is estimated that 74 percent of them occur in fifteen- to twenty-four-year-olds. Controversy over sex education erupted over the CDCP report. President Cecile Richards of the Planned Parenthood Federation of America charged that the report proved that "the national policy of promoting abstinence-only programs is a $1.5 billion failure, and teenage girls are paying the real price." Sex education must be offered to teenagers, but the way to teach it should be effective instead of titillating and pro forma. Health dangers as the CDCP found should be fully covered. However, I recall that chaplains' lectures on VD dangers when I was a Korean War GI had little effect on soldiers' promiscuity. Since the power of the sex urge is not easily curbed, education and example have tough roles to play. Because young people lead in sexually transmitted disease statistics, the manner in how they are raised and taught can make all the difference. On this and other health concerns, families, schools, and community agencies should find ways to work cooperatively together.

Famed social psychologist, Kurt Lewin, a Jew who escaped Nazi Germany by coming to America, believed that social relations determine people's behavior and lives. He conducted a landmark study of four different management styles on groups of boys that parallel what this chapter discusses. Lewin's study included a filming that demonstrated how four different management styles affected the boys' behavior and work effectiveness. When available at campus audiovisual centers, I often showed that film to my education and psychology classes. Let's begin to discuss the three managing styles to avoid with the very worst approach.

Neglectful-Indifferent Style

Neglectful caregivers pay little attention to their children and are apathetic toward them. Perhaps out of joblessness, drugs, physical and mental disability, etc., they give little care and time to their children and are unconcerned about their activities and interests. Their youngsters do about whatever they want and discipline is nil. The household could resemble a rundown hotel, with caregivers and children all going their own ways. They may live in squalor as a family I knew—trash and dirt littered filthy floors covered over with cardboard. When I taught at the University of Texas, Austin, I learned that some children from wealthy families who attended the university's prestigious laboratory school spoke in a lower-class manner, like the servants who cared full-time for them while the neglectful parents traveled far and wide.

It is doubtful that there are many neglectful teachers in public schools, but any will not be employed very long since their classes could be bedlams at worst and do-nothings at best. When new to teaching, I was told that the most important policy for teachers was to be in full control of their classes and that maintaining discipline was the most important expectation of principals. The question is: how is control handled? While indifferent teachers may not be neglectful to the extent that they cannot control their classes, they may do nothing more than go through the motions, minus meaningful teaching and relations with students. I had a middle-school teacher who assigned a chapter to read in the textbook at the beginning of each class and sat silently at her raised desk through the hour. Because we "Depression babies" were reared to comply and conform, she got away with her stony-faced indifference.

Although the popular image of military discipline portrays soldiers' strict attention to duty and obedience, indifferent neglect has occurred. During the War of Independence and the War of 1812, when civilian militia outnumbered regular, trained troops, the militia as individuals and entire units did whatever they wanted, often deserted, and fled before the enemy. Because militia officers were elected and held rank at the pleasure of their troops, militia commanders often treated orders from above with willful indifference, which was why General Washington desperately implored the Congress to authorize funds to raise and train a proper army. However, his appeal to patriotism and offers of bonuses helped to maintain a skeleton army in the worst of times. As a professor, my patience grew thin with neglectful and indifferent students and colleagues who did their own thing, with little respect for responsibilities.

Concerned only with themselves and their affairs, neglecting, indifferent, and laissez-faire parents are the worst possible guardians of children. Worse than indifferent teachers in the confines of schools, apathetic parents can endanger children's basic needs, safety, and health. Fending for themselves, neglected children fall into delinquency and become impulsive, crude, and inconsiderate of others. Characterized by immaturity, self-interest, and inability to accept responsibility and adult direction, they often mess with alcohol, drugs, sex, and crime. Reaching adulthood, products of neglectful backgrounds are prone to be in trouble with the law and/or live on the edge as among the homeless. If they attend school, they can stretch teachers' patience with their antisocial attitudes and habits. As a series of PBS' News Hour reported in 2008 on schools in New Orleans and Washington, D.C., school systems become dysfunctional when students lack discipline and learning readiness, and teachers are reduced to indifference because they cannot or are unwilling to cope with such unruly students.

Authoritarian-Dictatorial Style

The opposite of neglectful types, authoritarian parents and teachers domineer children with coercion and demands. Dictating strict obedience, they allow little individuality ("My way or the highway!"). Authoritarians force children to conform to their will through shame, guilt, and punishment. Throughout history, youths have been indoctrinated through constraints and rewards for conformity. In World War II, for example, German boys who had been thoroughly trained to rigid conformity became Adolf Hitler's prized troops as adults. Perfectly manipulated by authoritarian dictates, those young men never developed character of their own. Viewing others in stark them-versus-us, hierarchical dimensions, tyrants portray their kind as superior to all whom they degrade. They sway children to think the same, as illustrated in the song, "You've Got to Be Carefully Taught," in the highly successful musical, *South Pacific*, on stage (1949–1953) and film (1958), by Richard Rodgers and Oscar Hammerstein:

> You've got to be taught to hate and fear,
> You've got to be taught from year to year,
> It's got to be drummed in your dear little ear–
> You've got to be carefully taught…
> You've got to be taught before it's too late–
> Before you are six or seven or eight,
> To hate all the people your relatives hate–
> You've got to be carefully taught!

When American media and war movies depict battle heroism, they praise individual warriors and units for their courage. Yet credit should also be given to military indoctrination and training, as obedience and conformity are drilled into soldiers. Authoritarianism distinguishes much of the military and its purpose. Analyzing my Korean War service in chapter three of my book, *Yeee-Hah!* (2005), I told how I complied with the U.S. Army's strict demands of me as a soldier, even when they seemed ridiculous. For example, officers instructed us basic trainees to immedi-

ately salute all autos we passed with the blue insignia of
an officer, whether anyone sat in the car or not. Drill sergeants punished us with push-ups for anything they didn't
like. Having each soldier equipped with a dinner knife,
our CO ordered us to get down on hands and knees and
cut a lawn clean. I had opportunity to ask a colonel about
that particular order and others. He replied that such
tasks kept soldiers busy. Therefore, it was most satisfying
to put stateside duty behind me, and serve where Korean
duties focused on necessity and reality.

Bayonet training was drilled into us recruits, as they
had us racing across fields fiendishly screaming, stabbing,
and slashing as warriors of old, just like cavalry hurtling
like thunder wielding their swords and lances. The thun-
derous, savage yelling supposedly terrifies the enemy to
flee and musters the chargers' primeval bloodlust.

> Into the jaws of Death,/Into the mouth of Hell./
> When can their glory fade?/O the wild charge they
> made!
> —Alfred Tennyson,
> *The Charge of the Light Brigade*, 1864.

Applauding my bayonet work, particularly the lunge, drill
sergeants called on me to demonstrate for the troops atop
a stage. They didn't know that I had been a trophy-win-
ning fencer at the University of California-Berkeley, and
were probably ignorant of the sport. Lunging with the
bayoneted M-1 rifle, however, is just the reverse of what
it was for me in fencing. A right-handed rifleman kicks
off of his right foot and lands ahead on his left. Right-
handed soldiers carry the bayoneted rifle on the right side
where their trigger finger is. Several times, I fooled the

unsuspecting drill sergeants by holding the rifle on my left side, and with the footing exactly like my proper fencing stance, I got off terrific lunges with prompt recoveries, which caused the sergeants to exclaim, "Yee, damned if that's not the best we've seen! Do it again."

In order to maintain some sense of balance, besides compliance in doing my best as a soldier, I also held what I called an objective, fly-on-the-wall point of view. On one hand then, I told myself *this is the Army and they are telling me what's expected of a soldier, so do and be that and I did as well as possible.* On the other hand, in my inner mind often in humor, I studied the military as an institution and privately entertained alternate courses of action, particularly when orders went askew. Those two approaches and the congeniality of my buddies helped me to endure three years of the military and maintain a good sense of balance. Similar to my dual approach to the military, film director Masaki Kobayashi related the experiences of a World War II Japanese conscript who was a pacifist in heart, but did his duty as well as he could. Satisfied in having been a good soldier for my country, I was happy to return to civilian life. However, I should say that a welcomed transfer from Korea to Japan prior to discharge proved to be a most delightful time of my life, since in civilian clothes, I could blend in and fraternize with the locals and wander about freely.

My lasting impressions of the Army are as follows: (1) how fast its training methods could turn civilians from all walks of life into warriors within months, but more in action than mind, (2) impersonal obedience to hierarchical authority, (3) great wastage of time, effort, and resources, and (4) soldiers' off-duty behavior and mind-set were

lowbrow and often boorish, which military authoritarianism induce with its "kill or be killed," either-or mentality. Despite the heroic esprit of popular war films, this
last point is verified by Michael Massing's summary of
GIs' off-duty behavior in his review of six books written
by U.S. soldiers who served in Iraq (*New York Review of
Books*, December 20, 2007, page 83): "Officers and enlisted
men alike take pride in their profanity...The soldiers
often fight with one another, tell dirty stories, use racially
tinged putdowns, read porn magazines, and masturbate."

Since America's armed forces sustain national security,
they are essential, but their regimentation and methods
are not meant to be the essence of a free and open society.
Having led the War of Independence to victory, George
Washington quickly cast off his military uniform and
scoffed at the idea that he should become America's king.
He was elected President of the Society of Cincinnati,
which took its name from Cincinnatus, the Roman who
quickly returned to farming after his successful general-
ship of several wars.

Generally moody, insecure, and dependent on their
masters, children with authoritarian personalities tend
to lack creative, original thinking, and communication
skills. Antisocial at school, they're liable to be tattletales
and troublemakers. If compliant and orderly, they can be
inflexible. It says much that belligerent militia and neo-
Nazis, whose modus operandi is hostility and violence
against those they hate, are typically school dropouts and
confused rabble with little or no sense of social and civil
realities. Close-mindedness and self-righteousness characterize authoritarians.

Consider the following anecdote. A tough, long-serving sergeant conducted his family and raised his many children just as he ran his soldiers, e.g., strictly by the book. Once a month, he held a session for his wife and children to come forward individually to report on their work and how they could improve. His wife came first and usually reported family needs, such as getting the children new shoes and problems with the kitchen stove. Starting with the oldest, the children reported, typically saying, "No problems, sir," just like good soldiers. One day, the youngest came before the sergeant father seated behind a desk and said, "Sir, I just want to know how I can transfer out of this no-good, chicken outfit."

In reality, without transfer procedures available as in the military, many young people run away from unbearable homes. Along with other unfortunate statistics regarding U.S. youth, the nation has more than 1.3 million homeless young people, 27 percent of the total homeless population. Living in squalid conditions on the streets and in abandoned buildings, they have no hope and go uneducated. Poverty, family disorder, and rigid authoritarianism drive many youths to escape by running away and live in homelessness. Many prostitutes come from such family backgrounds.

The U.S. Centers for Disease Control and Prevention issued a gruesome report in 2008 that said that one of every forty-three American infants (91,278 out of 905,000 children of all ages) is physically abused or neglected. Babies are at tremendous risk during the first weeks of their lives. Ileana Arias, who leads the Centers' injury-prevention activities, bemoaned the crude pattern of many parents in harmfully beating, kicking, burning, and shaking children, and fail to provide basic food, shelter, and clothing. Indicating that child abuse is nothing new in the U.S., the findings for 2006 are the same as in 2002. In late 2009, the U.S. Department of Health and Human Services released its latest report on U.S. child deaths due to maltreatment. While an annual rate of about fifteen hundred reported child abuse deaths for each of the years from 2003 to 2006 is appalling, the 2009 report said that the rate skyrocketed to 1,760 in 2007. Child abuse deaths appear to be increasing at a frightening rate during America's great recession, as highlighted by 2009's partial-year doubling of thirty-seven deaths versus all of 2008 in Nevada's Clark County, where Las Vegas is located. In 2003, UNICEF calculated that the child abuse rate in America was three times higher than Canada's and eleven times higher than Italy's. Mean, dictatorial households are typically impoverished. A report by the National Academy of Science in 2009 found that 47.4 million Americans lived in abject poverty, compared to the figure of 39.8 million reported by the U.S. Census Bureau, both very high.

Discussing his state's drive to stem the use of methamphetamine, Montana's Attorney General Mike McGrath lamented in 2008 that "half of all children in the state's foster care system were there because their parents had abused or neglected them while high." According to the Nemours Foundation's Web site, the Shaken Baby Syndrome (SBS) can dislodge and damage babies' brains permanently. It said, "Approximately 60 percent of shaken babies are male, and children of families who live at or below the poverty level are at an increased risk for SBS, as well as other types of child abuse." Poor, young men living temporarily with the babies' mothers were the leading culprits of SBS. Confronting abuse data alone, we should not wonder why the nation's prisons are overcrowded and half of the high school students in the fifty largest cities never graduate?

William C. (Bill) Pack, prize-winning writer (*Bottom of the Sky*), was born in a rural Montana mining town where he grew up in an home environment beset by addiction, abuse, poverty, and mental illness. He said that the courts emancipated him from his parents at age fifteen, and a year later he dropped out of high school, married at seventeen, and became a father at eighteen. After working variously as a truck driver, a bartender, a fry cook, a dockworker, and a broadcast ad-man, at twenty-one he began a successful career as a broker with Merrill Lynch in Billings, Montana. From there, he advanced to Silicon Valley and well-being. At forty-eight, he enrolled as an undergraduate at Stanford University and won acclaim in archaeology after his graduation. Pack's life story shows that while parents' neglectful and dictatorial traits can produce troubled youths, a few of whom like Bill Pack can fortunately put themselves together and succeed in life. However, prospects for the great majority of children raised in mean environments cannot be expected to be as bright, such as the four-year-old girl whose father waterboarded her in Tacoma, Washington in early 2010. Because she couldn't recite the alphabet and he knew the girl feared water, the father used the torture technique.

Indulgent-Permissive Style

Except for the big difference of caring or not caring for their children, the management style of permissive parents and teachers resembles the neglecting-indifferent style. Rejecting power and coercion, indulgent-permissive types allow their children great freedom "to be only themselves." Indulgent caregivers believe that the natural impulses of youth are healthy and beneficial to their greater being if given ample opportunity to emerge. They reason that their lenient approach will raise and teach children who will be self-confident and creative.

The French philosopher, Jean-Jacques Rousseau published *Emile* (1762), a famous book about raising children. He wrote that children are born wholesome, and it is society and the company they keep that corrupts. Rousseau's ideas, therefore, match the belief of permissive caregivers to let children grow and learn naturally of their own accord, like wildflowers in the field. He believed that children were born perfect organisms that were ready and eager to learn from their environment, preferably in the country away from the corrupting influences of the city and its institutions. Chastised for his gross hypocrisy, Rousseau fathered five children out of wedlock with an illiterate maid, all he shamefully sent to an orphanage for foundlings.

Homeschooling.

According to the U.S. Department of Education, homeschooling involved 1.1 million American youths in 2003 and probably more today. With home-study curricular material that are available on the Internet and from homeschooling groups, home study has been used for long by families overseas and in areas far from schools, as by Sandra O'Connor when a girl. It also appeals to families that have reason to dislike their public schools and/or want their kids to learn a faith-based curriculum. Some home-school their children so the kids can work during the day and supposedly study at night. Then there are those who use home-study material to supplement schoolwork in subjects that may interest or trouble a youth, a reasonable practice. As a graduate student, I pored over several textbooks of the same subject to see how different authors explained certain complex topics and methods. No one textbook should be viewed as complete and final.

In August 2008, the California's Second District Court of Appeals overturned its earlier decision that state law required that homeschooling parents send the state's estimated 166,000 children, aged six to eighteen, to full-time public or private schools, or have state-credentialed tutors teach them at home. The California Teachers Association, the largest state teachers union, was highly disappointed with the decision. Its attorney said, "Parents do not have an unfettered right to dictate the terms of their children's education. Unregulated, unsupervised homeschooling is an invitation to 'educational anarchy.'"

The case had been initiated by three of eight minor children, the oldest accusing their father of "physical and emotional mistreatment." All eight children were home-schooled at home by their mother. The parents justified their not sending their children to school with reasons, such as religious beliefs and not believing in the policies of the public schools. Objecting "to his children being taught in school about evolution and homosexuality," the father added that educating children outside the home exposed them to "snitches."

In January 2010, a Tennessee judge granted asylum in the U.S. to a German family with five children, aged two to twelve. The parents argued that they feared punishment for homeschooling their kids in Germany, a nation that mandates that children attend an officially recognized public or private school to promote social integration. Fervent Christians, the parents claimed that the German schools were unruly and that school textbooks included stories of devils, witches, and disobedient youths. Anxious that the case could encourage a wave of asylum seekers on the basis of homeschooling, U.S. immigration authorities are appealing the judge's ruling.

Unschooling is a radical form of homeschooling that rests on permissive sentiments. As the *John Holt and Growing Without Schooling* website explains,

> I define unschooling as allowing children as much freedom to learn in the world, as their parents can comfortably bear. The advantage of this method is that it doesn't require you, the parent, to become someone else, i.e., a professional teacher pouring knowledge into child-vessels on a planned basis. Instead you live and learn together, pursuing questions and interests as they arise and using conventional schooling on an "on demand" basis, if at all. This is the way we learn before going to school and the way we learn when we leave school and enter the world of work…Unschooling, for lack of a better term (until people start to accept living as part and parcel of learning), is the natural way to learn. However, this does not mean unschoolers

do not take traditional classes or use curricular materials when the student, or parents and children together, decide that this is how they want to do it.

Unschooling assumes sensitive, knowledgeable caregivers who are close by their children most or all of the time. Unschooling literature suggests that adherents are advantaged and enjoy enriching settings. Togetherness, an oft-expressed, sweeping slogan of the past, meant being intimately close to one's children and at their beck and call. It faded because few caregivers had the luxury and patience of devoting constant attention to their young, especially the employed. Yet, some active togetherness is popular— travel, innovative games, community facilities and events, and equipment, such as back and front harnesses, hooded cycle-drawn carts, and running perambulators. Given the choice, however, it would seem that most teenagers would probably prefer the TV and PC to a constant diet of intimate dialogue and activity with their caregivers.

Unschooling leaders, such as John Holt, appear to be as child-centered as Rousseau. They speak of children learning through their own initiatives and interests, such as their suddenly getting excited with hot rods and studying all there is to know about auto mechanics, history, etc. Such thoroughness of interest and study by youths is doubtful. Unschooling seems to be pure indulgence. Question: How do indulged, unschooled children learn the basic three-Rs with real skill and understanding? An answer comes from the failure of discovery math education.

On September 12, 2006, the National Council of
Teachers of Mathematics (NCTM), a society of one hundred thousand educators from preschool through college,
completely reversed itself in declaring that "schools should
focus heavily and early on teaching such fundamentals as
multiplication tables and long division." In 1989, when the
NCTM decided to support "open-ended problem solving
over drilling," traditionalists clashed with "discover learning" educators. Debra J. Saunders (*San Francisco Chronicle*,
June 22, 2008) characterized the "Math Wars" in California as follows:

> On one side stood educrats, who advocated
> mushy math—or new-new math. They sought to
> deemphasize math skills, such as multiplication
> and solving numeric equations, in favor of pushing
> students to write about math and how they might
> solve a problem. Their unofficial motto was: There is
> no right answer. (even to 2 + 2.)
>
> They were clever. They knew how to make
> it seem as if they were pushing for more rigor, as
> they dumbed down curricula. For example, they said
> they wanted to teach children algebra starting in
> kindergarten, which seemed rigorous, but they had
> expanded the definition of algebra to the point that
> it was meaningless.
>
> On the other side were reformers (traditionalists),
> who wanted the (State) board (of Education) to push
> through rigorous and specific standards that raised
> the bar for all California kids. Miraculously, they
> succeeded, and they took pride in the State Board of
> Education's vote for academic standards that called
> for all eighth-graders to learn Algebra I.

Therefore in 2006, seventeen years after it had decided for new math, the NCTM reversed itself and called for a return to basics. Besides facing up to the poor math achievement of American youth, the change made use of what has been known for long about learning and memory. Francis Fennell, then NCTM President, said that unlike students in Asia, the increasing number of U.S. college students needing remedial math training had reached alarming levels.

In Singapore, where students have outperformed in international math tests, its schools concentrate children's work and attention on structured math topics, such as multiplication, division, and algebra with steady, daily practice. They build on that by learning formulas and solving increasingly difficult problems. That contrasts sharply with the now discarded discovery approach in the U.S., which the (Council's) report noted has long been described as "a mile wide and an inch deep." Stanford University math professor R. James Milgram criticized "fuzzy" math by saying, "There's increasing understanding that the math situation in the U.S. is a complete disaster." Reform-minded educators, such as Terry Bergeson, then-Washington State's Superintendent of Public Instruction, said the revision is a return to "balance." It took so long to reverse because many caregivers and educators, like the nature-child notions of Jean-Jacques Rousseau, believe that youngsters should be raised and taught to develop on their own. As in other areas of life, such as politics, ideology can override reason.

Although the NCTM's decision to return to basics confirmed those who opposed free and loose, discovery-teaching methods for math and other three-R tools, the fact that it took seventeen years for the correction is appalling. Teachers and school administrators, who allowed ideology to blind their objectivity, betrayed students, profession, and America. Permissive educators have found it unworkable to teach spelling and handwriting to pupils through "discovery" methods, which should have been obvious from the start. Parents should have spotted their children's three-R weaknesses, and they must share responsibility because of their blind reliance on the schools and lack of involvement. Fed up with fuzzy math and unstructured language studies, more and more parents enroll their children in private tutoring, such as Kumon, a math and language tutoring firm with more than nineteen million students worldwide.

The *New York Times* (Susan Saulny, November 26, 2006) provided insight into unschoolers' thinking. One mother interviewed for the article said:

> Much of the basic mathematics that (her) daughters have learned so far, she said, sprung from their desire to calculate how much allowance money they would have to earn to buy dolls featured in their favorite toy catalog. Each child gets a small weekly allowance that is deposited directly into her own bank account, then the adding and multiplying begins. The lessons have inadvertently, and painlessly, extended to taxes, shipping fees and postage, which she sees as another benefit of unschooling.

That anecdote could be an example of supplementing true math lessons, but it is hardly an adequate substitute to classroom or home-study learning. Having kids learn math and other three-R basics through vicarious happenstance, as the NYT article reported, shortchanges children's knowledge and ill-prepares them for high school, college, and employment opportunities in the future.

The Progressive Education Association (PEA).

The leading exponent of indulgent-permissive education through most of the 20th century, the PEA was first organized in 1919 to crusade for a learner-centered approach to education. Its adherents were inspired by John Dewey (How We Think, 1910; Democracy and Education, 1916; Experience and Education, 1938) and by other philosophers and psychologists through the twentieth century. Calling for pragmatic, critical thinking education in complicated, scholarly language, Dewey and other thinkers condemned rote, subject-oriented education and said children's interests and their active involvement in learning should be given greater attention. Extolling oversimplified interpretations of what Dewey and others said, PEA ideology enjoyed strong support among elementary school and teacher educators.

After decades, however, PEA battle cries, such as "learning by doing," "democratic teaching," "child-centered learning," and "creativity" sounded increasingly hollow and starry-eyed. This was especially so after Rudolf Flesch published Why Johnny Can't Read, a 1955 bestseller that rocked the nation with its harsh criticism of the Progressive Movement's feel-good, unstructured teaching methods. Flesch published more books on phonics and language usage, such as How to Write Plain English (1979) and Life English (1983). Replacing the PEA, the Progressive Education Network holds biannual conventions.

Before the progressives began to lose their grip on U.S. schools, educators would incant slogans as if they were spiritually self-evident. In education meetings that I attended as a new teacher, "creativity" was spoken in almost every sentence. As Dewey and other educational philosophers attacked the progressive movement for distorting their ideas, conservatives, cartoonists, and back-to-basics groups ridiculed PEA's pop psychology and free-wheeling liberalism. In a movie I once saw, a lad enrolled in a progressive school said that much of his and other children's time at school was spent running through a big hoop that supposedly symbolized their birth. It exaggerated PEA's permissiveness and pop psychology, but it hit home. Conservatives in the "Return to Basics" camp were equally outspoken, as they demanded that reading should be taught solely through phonetics and revival of the McGuffey Readers, a nineteenth-century bestseller series with racist tones.

Instead of thrusting irrelevant wish-for bromides on to children, educational programs should be pragmatic, results-oriented, and worthy of children's futures. International tests of children's learning have completely unraveled the claims of progressives that their methods produce high achievement. The tests showed that U.S. students scored far below students of foreign nations, who were taught through structured curricula, as chapter six covers.

As the PEA rightfully condemned the rigid rote methods of the past, there have been progressives who were somewhere between indulgent-permissive and author-itative-engaging styles of teaching children. Adopting Wikipedia's list of what the Progressive Movement accomplished, in my opinion, the good that came out of the PEA Movement has been:

1) School curriculum today is more flexible and student interests really matter.

2) Teachers are viewed as facilitators of learning who encourage students to use a wide variety of activities to learn.

3) Teachers encourage both individual and group study.

4) Valuable learning resources can be found in community agencies and active service programs and projects.

My own educational philosophy and practices include that list, but there is much more to education. My criticism of progressive education is that it concentrated on indulgent freedom of choice based on a here-and-now, good-feel benevolence. As it paid poor attention to three-R facts and skills learning, it showed little concern for preparing children for their futures. Also, PEA's them-versus-us rhetoric typically resided in nebulous slogans.

As for indulged-permissive children educated strictly through unschooling at home, their prognosis is questionable, as they will face diverse people and conditions, unlike their protective households. Life is not a snug sanctuary imbrued with caregivers' lenience and love, especially in today's no-nonsense world where advanced know-how and skills are valued. Psychologists have found that permissive childrearing in exacting form generally produces people who cannot control themselves well and expect to get their own way all the time. As adults, their impulses and emotional highs and lows promote difficulties with others, particularly those closest to them, followed by profuse apologies and pledges to shape up. Their urge for instant gratification can lead to problems with alcohol, drugs, gambling, and worst. When stymied, indulged children often throw temper tantrums and blame others for their own faults. They tend to be unpopular with other youths because of their social ineptness and their inability to share and recognize limits. Disrespectful of others and their property, they fail to take responsibility for their actions. It goes to show why such children tend to be poor spouses.

Advocating happy, sound marriages, Father Pat Connor of Bordentown, New Jersey has counseled countless numbers of girls for forty years. He advised,

> Never marry a man who has no friends. This usually means that he will be incapable of the intimacy that marriage demands. I am always amazed at the number of men I have counseled who have no friends. Since, as the Hebrew Scriptures say, 'Iron shapes iron and friend shapes friend,' what are his friends like? What do your friends and family members think of him?

The behavior of neglected- and indulgent-raised children seem a bit similar, but indulged youths could be more civil since they have had the advantage of interaction with close ones. While neglecting parents do not establish much or any attachment with their children, permissive parents form attachments with their youths that are highly personal with little probable carryover to others.

Several years ago, a mother in Pennsylvania was arraigned for buying her troubled son, who had Columbine-like symptoms, all sorts of weapons, including explosives, for no reason other than to indulge him. John

W. Santrock's textbook, Psychology (1991), presented a bizarre example of indulgent upbringing that is both amusing and pathetic:

> One boy whose parents deliberately reared him in a permissive-indulgent manner moved his parents out of their bedroom suite and took it over for himself. He is now 18 years old and has not learned to control his behavior; when he can't get something he wants, he still throws temper tantrums. As you might expect, he is not very popular with his peers.

Possible Shifting of Styles

As they portrayed the four managing styles of children, developmental psychologists have characterized them as being discrete and separate. But it is likely that there are overlapping mixtures and conversions from one style to another, since people and their circumstances are changeable and they can shift wholly or partly in how they affect children. Let's consider some of the possible shifts.

The indulgent-permissive style of fostering minimal control over the young opens the way for several possible changes.

Out of illness, divorce, or other family crises, permissive parents can become indifferent and neglectful. The essential presence and patience of indulgent parents and relatives may not be the same or readily available, which their children might misunderstand and resist. Although indulgent types believe that they want to boost their children's independence, their very permissiveness makes youths highly dependent on them. Minus their parents' and relatives' intimate presence, around which the children's activities and sense of well-being revolve and gain approval, the children could feel abandoned and neglected, and become hostile or passive. To lessen that possibility and enlarge their children's social relationships, indulgent caregivers should take turns with each others' broods and come together frequently.

Permissive parents and teachers can also shift to being authoritative engagers. That could happen when they feel that their children require more guidance and instruction than they are getting. Since the line between all of the styles lies on control and what is regarded as proper child behavior, some permissive types might decide that more rules and guidance would enhance household harmony and the youngsters' learning. That realization could come about with children that lack initiative and interests, or the opposite when youngsters are highly active and inquisitive beyond their ability, in which case caregivers decide that they can't cope, had enough, and turn to the schools. Permissive teachers might realize that they must be more structured to accord with curricular scope and sequence and/or told to do so by their principals. Perhaps influenced by friends and neighbors, youths might demand that they be allowed to go to school. Instead of constantly staying home, teenagers might want secondary schooling to be with pals and for the social and athletic activities. Facing higher education, unschooling youths will not have school-earned grades, etc., to include in admission applications, especially to prestigious universities. It would be interesting to compare the scores of unschooling youths on the SAT and ACT against national norms.

As for neglectful-indifferent caregivers, suppose they wake up to possible problems and misbehaviors of their children.

That might happen on a trip to visit relatives when they are packed together in the car and parents see how their kids conduct themselves before the relatives. Shock with their children's language and manners might cause caregivers to face reality and assess their neglectful child rearing. Or it could be the crisis of a youngster being arrested, harming another youth, or expelled from school that jolts their parents out of their indifference.

I have seen parents who have been so totally consumed by their work and businesses that they left their children to themselves after telling them to go to school, be good kids, and handing over money for their fast-food supper. Coming home late, those parents only saw their children briefly at night and retired exhausted from their daily grind. Some families I've observed hired a lady who washed and tidied up the house but had no responsibility over the children's conduct. When the parents realized their kids' waywardness, they either sent them to boarding schools or limited one parent's outside work so he or she could attend to the brood. Neglectful child raising probably occurs more often from parental outside commitments, especially work, than coming from abject indifference. Parents who wake up to the results of their neglect typically turn to tough authoritarianism, which teenagers reject out of hand

Writing about families with children who exhibit mental disorders, Benedict Carey (*New York Times*, December 22, 2006) reported that psychiatrists are rethinking and modifying drug-based therapy. Beginning in the 1960s, many psychiatrists blamed parents, usually mothers, for their youths' behavioral problems, such as neurosis, schizophrenia, etc. Defining the disorders as problems of brain chemicals that arose from household disarray, they prescribed drugs, which provided relief but little or no cure, such as Ritalin for attention-deficit hyperactivity disorder. Studies in the last decade have convinced many psychiatrists that some parental styles of raising children can also cause child mental problems. As Carey wrote,

> The science behind nondrug treatments is getting stronger. And now, some researchers and doctors are looking at how inconsistent, overly permissive or uncertain child-rearing styles might worsen children's problems, and how certain therapies might help resolve those problems, in combination with drug therapy or without drugs.

Because both styles raise children with personality and social problems, permissive-indulgent and neglecting-indifferent styles are under the microscope. Carey reported that studies by Dr. John March of Duke University and Dr. Oscar Bukstein at the University of Pittsburgh indicate that parents' adoption of what this book calls the authoritative-engaging interaction style brought about significant improvements with lower drug dosages or none. As one mother said about her attention-deficit hyperactive child, who threw "anything that could be launched" at home but was mild and friendly at school:

> People are so stressed out, and it's so much easier to say, 'Here, take this pill and go to your room; leave me alone'...But what I would say is that if you are willing to take on the responsibility of extra

parenting, you can make a big difference. I compare
parenting to driving. We all learn pretty quickly how
to drive a car. But if you have to drive a Mack truck,
you're going to need some training.

Dr. Gabrielle Carlson of Stony Brook University, whose
son had been diagnosed with attention-deficit hyperactivity, said the authoritative-engaging approach that she
adopted with good results required a "complete lifestyle
change," since she had to interact with her son instead of
giving him drugs.

*Dictatorial caregivers and teachers could shift to
the authoritative-engaging style, as Baron von
Trapp did through Maria's positive presence and
personality.*

A useful advantage of having more than one caregiver in
a family is the possibility that each adult will have his/
her own views on how children should be raised. Social
psychologists found that highly involved groups have
two types of leaders: one that tends to be the leader and
decision-maker, and another leader who is conciliating
and sympathetic to everyone's needs and feelings, as well
shown in chapter five's characterization of Henry James
Jr.'s father and mother. How the two leaders harmonize
each other's aims and interests can make or break a group.
Team-teaching provides such benefits and more. Dictatorial caregivers can shift towards other styles as kids mature
and resist what they argue against as unreasonable. As
American teenagers can often be hard to manage, hard-
line parents can be forced to adjust to youths who have

become less compliant and home-centered as when they were tots. Inflexible one-sidedness can lead to teenagers' sassy mockery as their interests and activities at school and elsewhere become more prominent than home. Faced with revolt and confrontation, autocratic parents and relatives who truly love their children will likely adjust, perhaps to be permissive and accommodating of their teenagers' desires and needs, or they could become authoritative-engaging, a harder shift. The latter could happen if there had been some leanings toward the engaging style when the kids were younger, in other words, some merriment and give-and-take social interaction. Authoritarians who shift to a permissive style surrender much of their authority, especially when their youths are teenagers who work and have money and wheels of their own. Such caregivers can maintain titular roles by providing congenial households and essentials, such as tuition funds.

As discussed earlier, the U.S. Centers for Disease Control and Prevention's 2008 report on family abuse of children indicates that youth victimization in America is a serious problem. It follows that neglectful and dictatorial caregivers, particularly poor and broken households, are most liable to child abuse. Another side of the picture is the increasing numbers of disoriented youths who suffer problems with alcohol, drugs, sex, crime, and indulge in Web thrills and pornography. Help for abused children can come through efforts of neighbors and welfare and community agencies, but their aid typically comes after serious abuse has been uncovered.

Most of the world's societies have traditions and cultures that avow authoritarian child raising, unlike modern-day America. Those nations' children have little choice but to comply as their parents and teachers dictate. But doctrinaire societies praise diligence and achievement, and they do not encourage senseless brutality. Authoritarian societies extend affection toward conforming children. Adolf Hitler's father was crude and brutal, but for his part, Adolf was exceptionally obstinate and resentful.

Authoritative-engaging caregivers could change to authoritarian-dictatorial

It could come about with engaging parents and teachers who leaned in the dictatorial direction and finally tired of reasoning with their youngsters. Maybe a family's growing number of children and mounting complaints and problems become burdensome and unwieldy. Since the chief differences between the authoritative-engaging and dictatorial styles are also how they handle control and what they regard as proper child behavior, engaging caregivers could become frustrated by time, health, and livelihood pressures. Exhorting their children at first, "Just do what I say; no argument. I'm tired," they get in the habit of making dogmatic demands. Authoritative-engaging teachers might fall into that out of frustration with boisterous, low-achieving students who don't respond to reasoning. Many hardworking teachers and principals have abandoned teaching altogether out of frustration with disruptive, weak students and inferior school and neighborhood environments. At infrequent times when my Windsor School pupils erupted into fights, reflecting their mean, depraved background, the thought crossed my mind, "I'm a grown-up, university graduate. What am I doing here?" Such misgivings would soon dissipate as the children responded to our class slogan, "Smart and good, that's me and us, today and tomorrow."

The temperamental tone of managing styles deserves consideration, for they can fluctuate from one to the other with swings in the mood of caregivers. For example, besides what was just said about authoritative-engagers shifting to a dictatorial style, there are would-be engagers who exhibit big highs and lows in mood occasionally or even everyday, such as less than momentary character shifts from adult mentor to buffoon playmate or ogre isolate. Gaudy tone shifts contradict the engaging style and should be avoided, as they confuse kids as to their caregivers' true nature and induce moodiness in them.

How children are raised and taught dramatically affects their mindset, behavior, and lives as adults. Of the four styles, because of its responsible, interactive nature and emphasis on children's preparation for their tomorrows, the authoritative-engaging style is the only one I and developmental psychologists recommend. As they confront social realities as adults, people raised strictly by neglecting-indifferent, authoritarian-dictatorial, and permissive-indulgent styles face adjustment difficulties that they may or may not be able to handle.

Psychotherapist Henry T. Stein, Director of the Alfred Adler Institute of San Francisco and Northwestern Washington, kindly gave me permission to reproduce the following outlines. Amplifying what this chapter and chapter two have discussed, Dr. Stein's two psychiatric charts add food for thought in how differing styles of raising and teaching children affect people's lives. His "Democratic Parenting Style" relates to what has been covered as the authoritative-engaging approach. Use of the term, "democratic," however, can mislead, as it did in the progressive education movement. Social interaction between children and their parents and teachers involves issue-oriented dialogue between adults and kids, such as the advisability of taking a bath and studying instead of taking a vote.

Dr. Stein's "Over-Indulgent" and "Over-Submissive" styles relate to what has been discussed as the indulgent-submissive managing style. Emphasizing more characteristics than what I have discussed under the authoritarian-dictatorial style, Dr. Stein's "Over-Coercive," "Perfectionistic," "Extremely Responsible," and "Punitive" parenting styles point out the dangers of close-mindedness and rigidity in people. His "Neglecting" and "Rejecting" styles are similar to what has been covered as neglecting-indifferent. Although the "Hypochondrical" and "Sexually Stimulating" styles are interesting, they are unrelated to our discussion.

What the reader should get from Dr. Stein's psychoanalytic charting is to see that there are many diverse, complex parenting and teaching styles, but only one that produces positive results in adult characteristics: his "Democratic Parenting Style," or what I commend as the authoritative-engaging style. My numerous observations of families and their children grown to adulthood verify the stylistic differences of rearing and teaching youth and the benefits and rewards of the authoritative-engaging style.

Adult Consequences of Childhood Parenting Styles

PARENTAL STYLE	ADULT ATTITUDE TOWARD LIFE	ADULT ATTITUDE TOWARD OTHERS	ADULT ATTITUDE TOWARD WORK	ADULT ATTITUDE TOWARD SEX & MARRIAGE
Democratic	Feels connected, part of life. Positive attitude. Willing to improve life.	Willing to help, share with, contribute to, and cooperate with others.	Work useful to others. Does his best to offer value. Can lead or cooperate on a team.	Sex as expression of mature love, caring, and giving. Feels equal to partner.
Over-Indulgent	Self-indulgent, bored, apathetic, restless, no initiative.	Passive expectation of getting from others. Expects them to anticipate his wishes.	Hates to work. Can't find a job. No career decisions, no preparation, or persistence.	Attaches to partners who indulge him. May use attractiveness or pretend weakness.
Over-Submissive	Very impulsive, hard to set limits, extravagant, has tantrums.	Used to getting own way, thoughtless of others' rights.	Impulsive, distractible, impatient, tyrannical. Expects admiration for modest effort.	Wants to be waited on, chooses a servant. Selfish, inconsiderate. Feels hurt if not catered to.
Over-Coercive	Divides life into "top dog" – "bottom dog" categories.	*Imitation*: becomes bossy. *Compliance*: a follower. *Internalization*: compulsive. *Rebellion*: refusal to comply. *Resistance*: procrastinator.	May be resistant to schedules and expectations, or may push self and others unmercifully.	Sex and marriage may be seen as duties and be carried out resentfully without satisfaction.
Perfectionistic	Life is a tedious chore, without color or sparkle. No pleasure in effort or result. Frequently depressed.	Unable to accept compliments. Feels superior to others who have lower standards. Can be critical and impossible to please.	May drive self to exhaustion. Must outdo himself, again and again. Overly concerned with detail. Never satisfied with work of self or others.	Usually unaffectionate, and unexpressive. Relationship may be too time-consuming. May search for "perfect" mate. Makes rules for performance.
Excessively Responsible	Super-responsible. Hard time letting-go and playing. Anxiety about relaxation. No mental refreshment.	Takes on excessive obligations, often depriving others of their share of responsibility or opportunity.	Always feels hard-pressed and driven. Fears everything would "go to hell" if he lets down. Can get stale with all work no play.	Never gets around to carefree times. Inability to relax and play with spouse or children.

PARENTAL STYLE	ADULT ATTITUDE TOWARD LIFE	ADULT ATTITUDE TOWARD OTHERS	ADULT ATTITUDE TOWARD WORK	ADULT ATTITUDE TOWARD SEX & MARRIAGE
Neglecting	Tends to be impulsive, filling life with compensation for a feeling of emptiness. Lonely.	Does not make close and meaningful contact. Superficial, exploitative relationships. Hides behind aloofness.	May strive compulsively after wealth, success, or fame to relieve feeling of emptiness. Stage performing may offer fantasy identities.	May yearn for partner to play a parent role, offering unlimited attention, acceptance, or affection. May be promiscuous, getting what he can from many.
Rejecting	Bitter, hostile, suspicious, and distant. May suffer from intense fears or anxiety. Feels worthless. May resort to substance abuse to relieve pain.	May see self as an outlaw, unacceptable to self and others. Very sensitive to rebuff. Suspicious, tests others with hostility and aggression.	Prefers working alone. May feel more comfortable with animals.	Starved for love, but expects rejection and provokes it. Has urge to hurt and reject others. Often attracted to unkind partners.
Punitive	Keenly feels injustice and longs for retaliation. Views world with envy and jealousy. Harbors a burning inner hatred. May feel "bad" and seek punishment.	May punish others who are smaller and weaker. May continue to act out whatever parents forbade. Can be excessively critical and self-righteous.	Can be attracted to harsh, aggressive occupations: police, army, boxing, football. May become ruthless businessman who "crushes competition." May punish self with excessive work.	May physically abuse partner. May engage in extravagant spending, drinking, speeding, fighting, and infidelity to punish partner. Often insanely jealous.
Hypo-chondrical	Constantly doctors self, doesn't feel well, and cannot participate in activities. Preoccupied with aches, pains, and disease.	Social life is restricted to those people who offer sympathy, service and indulgence. Likes others to call or visit and listen to his misery.	Frequently absent from work. Does barely enough to hold job. Work is felt as a burden to be endured, hardships are exaggerated.	Often prevents marriage. Mate is seen as a sympathetic doctor or nurse. Sex is often painful or curtailed. Unable to do housework, cooking, and shopping.
Sexually Stimulating	Tendency to over-sexualize many aspects of life or reject it entirely.	Preoccupied with sexual attraction and experience. May devalue friendship and non-sexual feelings for other sex.	Sexual attractiveness may be used for profit or influence.	Preoccupation with physical aspect of sex. Emotional intimacy and love is avoided. Partner is used to trigger fantasy. May act out rage against partner

To raise a newborn baby to the age of seventeen takes 6,214 days or 888 weeks. American youths attend school for about 180 days per year, much less than in other nations. In all that time with expenditures as mentioned earlier, children undergo tremendous physical growth and change as parents, relatives, and teachers impact their development in personality and mind. As this chapter has shown, there are many ways to go wrong. Wisdom calls for a well-rounded strategy and sensible tactics to make the most of children's youth and futures.

CHAPTER FOUR

LEARNING HOW TO LEARN AND THINK

> The thirst to know and understand,/ A large and
> liberal discontent;/ These are the goods in life's rich
> hand,/ The things that are more excellent.
> —Sir William Watson, *Collected Poems*, 1905.

Because of the children, my seven years teaching at three
elementary schools were my happiest as an educator. During my many years as a professor, few university students
equaled the kids' eagerness to learn, but three weekly lecture periods per course could hardly compare with having the kids five full days each week. With the children's
open-eyed curiosity, I could stimulate their thinking and
awareness by engaging their minds through social interaction, as this chapter illustrates. Caregivers maximize
success with children by having a strategy of solid goals
and reliable tactics to achieve them. The first and most
vital goal is establishing a positive relationship with children—MAC (Mutually Assured Connectivity) attachment
and social interaction through the authoritative-engaging
style of managing youngsters, as discussed in chapters one
and two.

Starting Up

Meeting a class of children for the first time, I sensed unknowns radiating in neon lights: "Who are you? What's our relationship?" First impressions arise when meeting strangers with little that should be taken as final. However, many people expose their naïve perceptions right off. For instance, my daughter, a professor of surgery, told me that patients often mistake her for a nurse. She said that she could take that calmly, since nurses are mostly females. She would tell them that she wasn't a nurse but could get them one. But when they say, "Your English is so good. How long have you been in the U.S.?" or blurt a nasty about "all these foreigners," she is frustrated. I told her, "Honey, just set them straight by saying, "I'm a fifth-generation American of Chinese descent." While most reply, "Why, you're more American than I am," and some bristle to reflect the gradation in the attitude complex, running from naïve ignorance to outright bigotry that I named the Asian Stereotype and analyzed in *Yeee-Hah!* (2005). Since youth, I have experienced the same many times. Merely on the basis of appearance, many have jumped to the rash conclusion that I wasn't an American.

Pupils didn't make the same error, except one boy on a first day who said out of turn, "When did you come from China?" Classmates immediately shouted, "Shut up, he's an American just like us!" Sensitive to stereotypes, I have studied them with much interest and believe that their persistence shows that the ethnic awareness of many people is limited. Why do ethnic, etc., stereotypes remain so prominent in a nation dedicated to pluralism and diversity? My answer is that many have not been properly raised and taught as children to meet people for the first time with courtesy and to refrain from prejudice.

Some information is available before the first day of school, such as the children's record files and their former teachers' comments, which I tried to ignore until I got to know the kids on my own. However, once a teacher rushed up to warn me of a boy in my new class who had been a hellion for her, such as blowing up condoms in class and casting them off into the air. Yet, the child never misbehaved in my class. As pupils wanted to get a handle on me, I wanted to initiate an air of openness during our first gatherings that would last. I introduced myself with basic information on my education, family, and teaching experience, and briefed the kids on our school rules and schedule. I explained my role as their friend and adult mentor and guide and when needed, their disciplinarian, which we discussed without disagreement. When I asked them what they thought their role as pupils might be, we discussed their pat answers about learning and being "good" kids. Filling the chalkboard with answers and refinements after spirited hand raising and responses, we analyzed them in order to distinguish between affectation, ideal, and reality and came to consensus on how all of us should work together. That round concluded when we achieved agreement on the fundamental idea that we should make the year as profitable and enjoyable for each and everyone as possible.

My primary purpose during those first days and weeks was for the class to begin to form sincere partnerships with me and each other. Heartwarming movies, such as "Mr. Holland's Opus," illustrate that goal. I repeated as their teacher, it was my job to enhance their learning and help them through our partnership to become bigger people with as much success and pleasure for all of us as possible. We reviewed the prescribed learning we had to cover in math, social studies, science, and language arts with the textbooks we had for those subjects. I said if we did well and proved to be efficient with the three-Rs as prescribed for them and some even surpassing the requirements, we could find time for special projects. Consensus gained from those highly involved discussions with much chalkboard drafts initiated the strategy for our work together, which we could refer to and build upon. I became proficient in writing on the board without losing eye contact with the kids, which was done to keep discussions going. If I ever misspelled a word, at times on purpose, they were to correct me. I appointed two pupils to write down our agreements from the chalkboard to serve as bylaws for later reference. Each day began with our outlining a schedule of activities on a chart, and ended with evaluation of what and how we did. If I had already taught at their school, pupils asked if they could have projects of past classes. This is mostly how I started the first days and weeks with fifth and sixth graders. Undoubtedly, primary teachers must be more directive with a motherly tone.

Many teachers have fond memories

of opening days at elementary schools. For example, word confusion is typical for many young children. For example, on the first day of school, a teacher I knew who was arranging the seating of her pupils told one girl, "Please sit here for the present." At day's end, the same little girl looked depressed as she passed the teacher, who asked her, "Is anything wrong?" The little girl replied, "Well, I sat there as you told me to and I never got the present you promised."

Something I also read went like this: A teacher with an ongoing unit on animals had a university researcher come to tell her pupils about his laboratory work with rats. He brought a cage of rats to illustrate his talk. As he was departing after his informative talk, the children thanked him. One said, "Yeah, we didn't know what a rat looked like before you came."

Here are three true stories of my own:

1. My first year of teaching was difficult, because I was a novice and had to learn fast from others and through trial-and-error. My job at rural Alexander Valley School was teaching the fourth-, fifth-, and sixth-graders in one room, which meant juggling lessons and reaching each pupil as best as I could. Group projects helped. When the fourth-graders were studying the California Indians, we decided to have a puppet play about their history. So we proceeded to make puppet heads. My flashbulb memory still sees the ten or so fourth-graders working around tubs of clay. One or two asked me what the Indians looked like. I reminded them that our social-studies texts had pictures of them, and also that we had studied how the Indians came originally from Asia across the Bering Strait. I said, "Indians have high-cheek bones like Asians. Look at me, I'm Asian." Taken aback, Danny Streeter said, "But we thought you were Mr. Yee."

2. Windsor School was the only school in one of California's poorest districts. The area housed impoverished families, many being refugees from Oregon's timber depression who had come south for better welfare support. Today, Windsor is a middle-class retirement and bedroom community, and Alexander Valley is known for its fine wines. A decade ago when I drove by the school, two pine trees that one of my classes planted looked strong and tall. My parents owned a tree farm and father gave me the trees. We planted them when we learned in a conservation unit that the U.S. downed more trees than were planted In that and other ways, I was determined to help the children gain hope and believe that they could improve their situation. While they may have found a different world at school and I would forget their dire poverty at home, something would jolt my senses to reality. For instance, pupils who had not attended for several days returned with mandatory written notes from a parent. One boy, who came back severely battered, had a note that said that he had been "bad" and was "spanked." A girl's note said, "Sarah missed school because we washed her dress."

3. My Frederic Burk School class took a field trip to visit a dairy and chicken hatchery near Petaluma in Sonoma County to help cumulate a unit we called, "Life and What It Is." We had hatched chicks in our own classroom. At the commercial hatchery, drums with controlled

heating and shelves of fertilized eggs hatched hundreds of chicks at one time. Above the front opening was a plate that identified the firm that had built the incubators, Robins & Co. One of the brightest girls came to me and said, "Where are the incubators for chickens?"

I recall from my own youth how children seek meaning and make errors and what they see that adults no longer see. When quite young going to school on my birthday, I was thrilled to see Santa Rosa's main drag lined with American flags on poles and thought to myself how very nice it was for the town to do that for me. Not bragging about it to anyone, I felt special since the town didn't do the favor for my brothers. It took several annual repetitions before I learned by reading the morning paper that my June 14 birthday coincided with Flag Day, and the flags on Fourth Street were not meant for me at all. That awakening wasn't a crusher, just one more incremental step towards reality. Busy probers of everything they come across, children see and approach the world from their own developing awareness and perspectives. Ask yourself if creek stickerback fish and the sheen of thin ice on puddles are as intriguing now as they were when you were a kid. Seeking to reach and guide children, one would do well to start where they are and try not to insult and trample upon their self-centered conceit.

A Great Job Opportunity

The last to learn about it, a dramatic change in my life occurred in 1959. Even affable Principal Phil Henry, who supported my projects, never breathed a word. San Francisco State College's Frederic Burk Laboratory School quietly reviewed me as a possible teacher. The school was named in honor of Frederic Lister Burk, celebrated President of San Francisco State Normal School. The institution became SFS College in 1921 and then to SFS University in 1972. After Frederic Burk's principal and others came to Windsor School to examine my teaching and classroom for final evaluations, their letter offering me a teaching job was received with "Yeee-Hahs!" As the salary doubled what Windsor paid me, a SFSC dean confided that FB teachers were paid more than starting assistant professors "because it's harder to find the teachers we want for Frederic Burk than assistant professors." With Irene pregnant with our first child, I completed my master's degree and teaching and administrative credentials that hectic summer before we moved to San Francisco. What a breathtaking leap it was to go from one of the state's poorest school districts with only four years teaching experience to teach at an internationally known, showcase institution! Transition from professor to graduate and research dean fourteen years later in 1973 was also momentous; however, the busy administrative work took me from teaching, and while it was responsible and challenging, it proved to be much less satisfying intrinsically.

San Francisco State professors from whom I had taken courses, especially those who had been curriculum supervisors in Sonoma County, must have recommended me. They and almost everyone else I worked with at SFS seemed enthused by a life force that sparked others to be all that they could become and made me feel welcomed. However, because SFS's facilities and budget did not support research, I moved to the University of Texas-Austin in 1964, which soon proved fortunate timing when the state, facing a funding crisis, closed Frederick Burk School.

Teaching at the famous laboratory school was never dull, since the school's mission was to demonstrate exemplary teaching methods and classroom environments. Our being handpicked as superior teachers, small and large groups of student teachers and educators from abroad came to observe our teaching and student response. Though visitations were usually scheduled ahead, a sudden call from the vice principal would ask if an out-of-town group, such as a party of twenty-five prominent Japanese educators, could come right over. Well-designed for the school's purpose, classrooms were fitted with unsparing touches, including benches built-in along half of the rear wall. Very large groups required extra rows of chairs. Although some visitations called for specific techniques, most groups came to see whatever my class was doing in art, science, language, and social studies. Hour-long visitations, which seemed like performances if one paid too much attention to the probing eyes and ears, could be tricky and even nervy at times; for like show business, the class and I were on stage. Unlike stage acting in the theater, however, though Frederic Burk teachers would have working scripts in mind, the pupils in my classroom played their roles with no prepping. What would Shakespeare's *Hamlet* be like if all characters, other than the Prince of Denmark, performed freely as they chose? However, experienced in having visitors throughout their years at Frederic Burk, the pupils paid little or no attention to the visitors. What Donald Schön has written about "reflection-in-action" and "reflective teaching" in general applies to my classroom teaching.

Unlike laboratory schools with select enrollments, such as John Dewey's famous, turn-of-the-century laboratory school at the University of Chicago, Frederic Burk's pupils came from the local neighborhood of middle-class families living in a private development of high-rise towers. Closed to nonwhites in those days before the civil rights laws, my family and I could not reside there with my pupils. I forced myself to ignore the racial bias as being impossible to do anything about. Yet, I felt well accepted, such as when a family asked if their daughter could stay with me another semester so she could graduate from high school in June instead of February. The housing authority allowed aquariums, but no other pets, and forbid walking and playing on the manicured lawns. Thus, the sterile residential environment meant that the school could play an enormous role in exposing the kids to the real world, which Frederic Burk staff saw as a great opportunity.

Igniting Love for Learning and Knowledge

I enjoyed teaching fifth- and sixth-graders, mostly sixth-graders, whom I cherished as alert, bright people. In their in-between formative period, fifth-graders are mostly quiescent and relatively easy to handle. A year later, with more mature brains and feeling spunky, sixth-graders could read and handle numbers as well as average adults if properly raised and schooled. The majority coming from downbeat families on welfare, Windsor children were underachievers, but the three-R skills of many mushroomed as they discovered the thrill of learning and what they could do with it. Joan, one of the brightest and hardest working pupils, mailed several five-by-eight book reviews weekly, long after the school year ended, which I returned with comments. Her mother, a county cartographer, told the class how pioneers had surveyed the land with long chains that they dragged across the land and that she had found old surveys that recorded distances by how many cigarettes had been smoked as men rode horses from one point to another. The pupils eagerly listened to what she told of the survey methods used by the pioneers versus today and the math involved. Compare that to a dry geography drill.

I made good use of resource teaching aides in my teaching. For another example, in relation to what we were studying about law and order, I invited a California Highway Patrolman to come and speak about his work. He arrived late with apologies and a grimy uniform and explained that he had just grappled with a serious auto accident. His words on law enforcement and all that it took to be a select CHP officer made a strong impression. During an aviation unit, an airline pilot spoke to the class, which included his daughter, about his training, love of flying, and the technology and concerns that ran through his head as he flew. He described how the city and bay of San Francisco; Mount Tamalpalis, just north of the Golden Gate Bridge; and Mount Hamilton, with the Lick Observatory to the south, provided pilots good landmarks, especially the two mountains that stood above the frequent fog of the Bay Area.

Demonstrating unrehearsed lessons for visitors, I never told my Frederic Burk classes any more than visitors would be coming at a certain hour. With learning and three-R skills objectives in mind, I believe that classroom teaching with or without visitors should be open to unplanned, useful elaboration, if not on the spot than to be picked up later. An art professor complimented me for initiating an art lesson with thorny shrubs and dried flowers by pressing my arm into thorns and uttering an "ouch," which, though unintentional, focused the pupils' attention.

During a reading lesson that an education professor had requested for his class, I rotated among groups of varying competence that were studying their respective workbooks and texts. I reached a group that had a story of a king's triumphant return from a big victory and his welcoming procession. As we discussed its new words, idioms, narrative style, etc., one boy simulated one of the buglers mentioned in the tale. Answering yes when I asked him if his move meant that he could immerse himself into the panorama, I asked his group to scan the story again and see if others could feel the same. Reading, being thinking and feeling at best, as SFS reading expert Larry Carrillo used to say, eager faces and comments showed that each group member could sense the boisterous scene and put themselves into it.

Taking advantage of the moment, I then asked each of the twelve or so to take the part of the story's many role players. One insisted there had to be a queen, even though the story did not mention one, so we added a queen. At the signal, for a grand moment while seated or on their feet by their chairs, they dramatized the proud king and queen, marching soldiers, the cheering crowd, buglers, and drummers by gestures and voice. Underlining one of

my chief themes, I reminded them and their appreciative classmates, who were listening in, that reading and
writing were means of communications that we should
try to master. I also pointed out that the story was quite
vivid at face level, and we should idenitify its underlying
assumptions and abstractions, whereupon they suggested
joy, patriotism, and pride, and I suggested nationalism
and the warm bliss of homecoming. Everyone, of course,
wanted a replay so the entire class could join in, but before
we did, for the benefit of the whole class, I had key passages of the story read aloud once again. The enthusiastic,
clamorous replay ended the lesson and demonstration. As
always, there was no opportunity for feedback from the
observers.

My Windsor School class also had visitors—officials
and curriculum counselors from the Sonoma County
Department of Education often came to observe lessons
and study the room environment. Since the kids had no
recurring experience with visitors, I didn't want them to
be distracted from lessons. So we worked up a simple, fun
greeting whenever visitors came. At my finger signal, every
pupil turned to face the visitor(s) and pointed to him or
her saying, "Welcome, friend!" After the acknowledgment
cleared the air, we resumed what we had been doing.

Social studies and science units were my favorite teaching areas, because of their unifying comprehensiveness,
and the open-ended teacher-pupil and pupil-pupil interaction that could spiral to wondrous learning and activity.
Besides the content, they provided much opportunity to
instill insights, raise awareness, and expand language and
math skills. To initiate interest, I enjoyed using colorful
room environments: bulletin boards on Frederic Burt's

cork walls, counter and table displays, and even piano wire that I strung high above desks to hang outstanding class work and holiday decorations. Teaching the same as at Windsor, I had banana boxes loaded with props and gadgets in the closet and at home, such as intricate airplane parts that the United Airlines maintenance personnel at SFO kindly gave me. I laid out parts, such as a lever in the wing fuel tank to help indicate fuel level, on a table with a poster asking what they were and how they worked in planes. The aviation display related to the after-hours model plane flying in the schoolyard, which many participated in with me and another sixth-grade teacher.

Initiating interest

I always initiated new unit studies carefully in order to gauge and develop pupil interest. I enjoyed the elaboration, as still a child myself prepping for Santa Claus. Initiation of a day's three-R lesson deserved attention, which took little time, such as a related joke or review of the previous lesson that stifled some pupils. Many teachers make the mistake of ignoring initiation altogether.

Wanting to spark and detect class interest, I said nothing about the aviation display and watched pupils discuss and manipulate the plane parts. Inquiries were sidelined by saying that we might discuss that later. If little interest developed, I would have dropped aviation and tried another topic; for the area of study was not as vital as learning objectives. After a week or so, discussion during our daily morning prep period led to a motion and unanimous vote to study aviation. A typical Frederic Burker, one boy said, "Mr. Yee, we know you want to have a unit on aviation and we're rarin' to go. Yeee-Hah!"

We began a combined social studies/science unit on aviation with preliminary readings and films. Afterward, follow-up inquiries and project proposals proliferated, which we listed and refined on the chalkboard. The elected class secretary recorded an agreed upon list of possible projects that committees might tackle. Lasting several weeks, the unit culminated with an earned field trip to San Francisco's airport, which included a thrilling tour of the control tower; no doubt impossible with today's security concerns. The sixth-graders became excitedly versed in many aspects of flight and space, types of air transport, and aerospace companies. Boeing and airlines responded to the children's letters by sending attractive and informative material on air control and passenger safety, international and domestic airlines and schedules, etc. They searched the school and public libraries for aviation-related books. If we had had computers and the Internet during my classroom teaching, the opportunities to access and seek information would have been greatly expanded. Although many elementary schools have computers today, they often remain idle, which may be due to constricted teaching and the lack of PC know-how. Some Frederic Burk pupils brought hand calculators to class, some quite sophisticated, that we used to calculate everything imaginable and, of course, practice and extend their math skills, which we pursued in regular structured lessons. After we had quizzes, out came the hand calculators to compute percentages of rights to wrongs and class proficiency, which I tabulated on the chalkboard for item analysis and discussion. Analysis highlighted the easy and hard quiz items to see if they were fair and adequate.

The number skills the sixth-graders used to plot distances and flight times between cities and nations helped to reinforce arithmetic lessons. Many pupils worked out their favorite flying schedules, and had a contest to see who could fly the furthest and also the fastest in one day from San Francisco. The original display exploded into many others that were researched, designed, drawn, and written by class committees, including instrument panels and controls of planes in paper crates, where they simulated operating as pilots taking off and flying. This demonstrated the importance of numbers in air speed, altitude, wind speed, etc., and in calculating flying time, distance, navigation, etc. All of this occurred during unit periods of about thirty to forty-five minutes most days, with a call to clean up in five or so minutes. Of course, pupils worked after school in the classroom and at home.

Some visitors probably viewed our classroom as cluttered, but we were orderly and made safety a priority. Problems occurred, from which we also learned as we solved them, as each day closed by assessing the day's work. Committee chairs would discuss progress and needs and tell on others, such as someone showboating during a visitation and those who failed to help clean up. Self-discipline comes from keen interest and group industry, but every class had at least one who sought mischief as a habit, such as the lad who connected a plane part to a wall socket and filled the room with white smoke. His frequent pranks led to his temporary suspension from school and a serious talk with his indulgent parents. Besides the depth of new knowledge gained, the three-Rs were enriched and made meaningful through the pupils' mostly self-directed readings, writing reports, and examining maps, the weather, and navigational math. No matter the unit, I learned as much as the children. Our slogan for the aviation unit was, "Know your stuff and fly right!" At day's end, I would ask, "Do we know our stuff and are we flying right?" The class replied with a resounding "Yes!"

With so much emphasis on standardized testing today, I worry that schools and teachers may not have the freedom and flexibility that we had and that teaching to tests is the rule. Diane Ravitch, a stalwart critic of U.S. education, believes that the No Child Left Behind law passed during the George W. Bush administration corrupts meaningful education through its excessive stress on tests. As long as we covered the State of California scope and sequence with its long lists of behavioral objectives, we could embark on social studies and science units that fitted pupil needs. Three-R studies were highly prescribed with state texts, which I taught daily and worked to integrate as much as possible for meaning and practice with the science and social studies units. We only had the annual California Achievement Test. Because a neighbor girl expressed great anxiety with tests two years ago, I suggested to the HS frosh and her mother that she enroll in a Kaplan test-taking course, which she did with good results.

The meaning and universe of life became another favorite unit that my classes explored. As we progressed, the classroom had several aquariums, both fresh and sea water; separate cages of hamsters, mice, and chicks (that we hatched in an incubator we built ourselves); a time-lapse camera filming plant growth; cupcake pans plugged with gelatin to grow molds (Professor Larry Carrillo thoughtfully warned me of breeding dangerous microbes); ten microscopes the SFS's science division kindly lent me;

and a proliferation of projects from the microscopic to dinosaurs and whales. With the microscopes, we watched chlorophyll coursing through plant veins in light and stopping in dark, and observed the intricacies of amoebas, fairy shrimp, flies, mold, etc. Pupils with written permission from home went with me after school in my VW "bug" to gather samples from tide pools and lakes. Extending activities beyond the classroom when possible, such real-life experiences help to open children's minds by stimulating a love for learning and the urge to question and find answers.

During the life unit, we read a chapter from a science textbook that Herman and Nina Schneider wrote. So fitting for us, what they wrote was inspired, no doubt, both being zenith types in their love of science and children. On one page, the Schneider's asked, "How old are you?" Their answer on the following page was: "As old as the saber-tooth tiger and as young as the morning dew on the rose." Smart as whips, most of the Frederic Burt pupils understood immediately. I can still see their excited faces and upraised hands, all eager to explain the riddle posed by the Schneider's. Yes, calcium and water have always been a part of the earth, and both are recycled constantly by nature. Thus, we are as old as the earth and as young as its constant regeneration and the cycle of life. That reading helped to initiate the life unit.

To have money to buy extra material and animals, we published a weekly paper that we sold to subscribers, who were mostly relatives. At home, I typed the children's articles onto stencils. One mother complained to me that we should not print copyrighted material, to which I could not convince her that everything was originally written by our pupils, but she left saying, "I can't believe that sixth-graders can write as well as that." After hours, class officers and/or committee chairs went with me in my VW to pet and hobby shops to find what we needed, and report back before the class gave approval to purchase. Because class officers had real and meaningful duties, including management of our funds, elections were big deals, which came three times a year.

Raising Class Funds

Far different from the Windsor children, the Frederick Burk kids had plenty of pocket money; their allowances exceeded my personal disposable cash. Jewish kids boasted that their parents' generosity extended to gifts for both Hanukkah and Christmas. When the idea of a class fund arose, the Frederic Burk kids said they could get all that we needed from home. However, discovering that they had never earned money on their own, I discussed with them how many kids their age made pocket money, such as delivering papers as I had. They leaped with eagerness to become entrepreneurs and after much discussion we decided to produce a weekly. At Windsor School, besides a subscription paper, we had cupcake and hot dog sales to raise funds for a Cinderella trip to San Francisco. One of my best friends, Alma Lauritzen, a concert impresario in the San Francisco Bay Area, helped us to secure tickets to attend a performance of Engelbert Humperdinck's wonderful opera, *Hansel and Gretel.* Driving to Windsor to teach us about the opera and the opera house, Alma admired their good singing and dancing and noticed that the girls were much bigger and taller than the boys, which is normal as girls mature earlier than boys. She also asked about a little girl who played jacks in isolation under the moved desk seats. I told Alma that she lived with a grandmother and suffered grieving depression since her parents divorced, and that I protected her with warmth and patience.

One Sunday, I made a practice run to San Francisco to find a park where we could lunch and use the restrooms and to map the route to the opera house after a tour of the city. On Principal Phil Henry's recommendation, the Windsor School board kindly provided us a school bus. It was the first trip to the big city for almost all of the kids, who also rode elevators for their first time in the splendid San Francisco Opera House. The Golden Curtain, the Golden Gate Bridge, skyscrapers, city sights, the opera, and area geography we had studied awed everyone. My Frederic Burk classes also went to the opera and enjoyed the experience with accompanying mothers, but being familiar with San Francisco's artistic and civic culture, their response did not approach the enthusiasm of the deprived Windsor kids.

Accumulating a big surplus in our Frederic Burk class treasury, we decided to solicit charities and invited them to make their pitch for donations. Letter writing being important in my classes, we mailed the one best letter in words and handwriting to whomever we targeted. Most charities replied by mail. Those that sent representatives to meet with us provided real-life experiences. Besides what the charities boasted that they did for the needy, we wanted to know the percent of funds they received that actually went to help people and how much was used for administration and solicitations. The *San Francisco Chronicle* newspaper reported our "no-nonsense" approach to charities.

My Philosophy of Teaching and Use of Examples

Teaching to me means helping pupils and students to get real insight into and practice of what they were learning, and thereby learn how to learn and think. Development of children's three-R knowledge and skills, attentive and objective awareness, clarity in framing and answering questions, and the ability and readiness to probe sources are vital for kids to take away with them and expand through their lives. As the metacognition theory ("knowing about knowing") of Stanford psychologist John H. Flavell states, thoughtful people have learned how to learn, think, reason, and process information before them and from their memory. Children should begin to learn how to do the same through varied, appealing approaches at home and school. Unlike olden times when issues and decisions were simpler, modern people must be equipped to handle complex systems and problems that are intertwined with multiple factors.

As David Brooks wrote (*New York Times*, May 27, 2010), the Deepwater Horizon oil explosion and mess was an example of poor "risk assessment" in our "ever-expanding array of intricate high-tech systems. These hardware and software systems are the guts of financial markets, energy exploration, space exploration, air travel, defense programs and modern production plants." And then there are the many complex issues of the economy, health care, politics, immigration, environment, communications, etc. More than risk assessment, security of situation and certainty of pertinent knowledge and possible good and bad outcomes are increasingly vital factors for each of us and the nation. For those in high office as in the government and corporations, absolute security and certainty are seldom knowable, even in probabilities as issues shift and are tackled. Those who stick their heads in the sand like ostriches and say none of that concerns them, stand on bias and blame, or make partisanship or a single issue their crucial end-all-and-be-all are like those who brought about the 1919 prohibition amendment to the Constitution and mid-19th-century Know Nothing Party who fought German and Irish Catholic immigrants. For children to mature to thinking adults in a democracy and developing world, their education must involve "knowing about knowing" and prepare them to deal intelligently with their complex society and world.

Like the lesson on million and billion which will come up soon, I often used concrete examples and stories to explain and flesh out concepts, as great teachers have done. The many parables (stories) that Jesus used to illuminate his teachings come to mind. His Good Samaritan parable makes the meaning and spirit of charity and humaneness abundantly clear. The concept would hardly hit home if taught in the abstract. When disciples asked him why he used parables to teach the people, Jesus explained (Matthew 13:15 KJB), because the peoples' understanding was so dull and hardened, so with parables "they should see with their eyes and hear with their ears and understand with their heart."

Teaching American university students in the 1990s, I confronted the poor learning attitudes and readiness of most; not a few had weak reading ability. Unlike the diligent U.S. students I taught in the 1960–70s, 1990's students, no doubt products of "discovery" education, treated studies with poor motivation and comprehension of abstract concepts. To get across major concepts, I often used stories, demonstrations, and even movie sequences to penetrate their thinking and memory. For example, I used to show two scenes from *The Boat*, an excellent 1985 movie of a World War II German U-boat. The first scene shown shows engineer Yohan going berserk during a frightful depth-charge attack. Irrationally, he struggled to flee the endangered sub. As the captain rushed away to get his pistol to stop him, others beat Yohan and dragged him away. In the second scene, later after his heroic efforts in the engine room, Yohan is shown reporting to the captain that the sub was saved from sinking. In reply, the captain smiled, patted Yohan on the back, and said, "Gut, gut, Yohan. Now go and get some rest." Afterward, I used the same words in a feigned German accent when students said something cogent to tease their memory. The points I wanted to stress with those scenes were MAC social reinforcement and the power of positive, sincere words and acts at the right moment to promote camaraderie, redress and reconciliation.

Dumbing Down U.S. Universities

Even though Hong Kong students I taught in the 1980's could ace tough multiple choice exams because of their dedicated study habits and amazing skill at memorizing, I also provided them the example approach to help extend their insight into and understanding of concepts. Students in East Asia advance from the lowest grades to higher education through strict discipline to memorize and master tests that U.S. students would find highly extreme. While 70 percent of U.S. college-aged students are enrolled in higher education, less than 20 percent of similarly aged Asian students are enrolled, and only a few can enter the most prestigious institutions.

Unlike the flexibility for American university graduates, in Asia what university one graduates from can be life-determining, because Asian universities are ranked by how difficult it is to be admitted and the institutions' record of graduates' employment and achievements. Believing that all bachelor's degrees are fairly equivalent, American students decide which schools to seek admission to by many nonacademic factors, such as location, buddy and romantic ties, sports, costs, etc. Although U.S. private universities are the most prestigious and hardest to enroll in, such as Harvard and Stanford that cost about $50,000 a year to attend, the very best universities in Asia are public, and their students are tuition-free and provided stipends. Private Asian universities are expensive and few in number.

Since each step up the highly select educational ladders of Asian nations depend on top exam performance, Asian youths cram tirelessly from primary school through the educational system and study extra harder months before university admission exams. It's unfortunate that Singapore and Germany separate the gifted from ordinary pupils as early as grade four with a life-affecting examination. While gifted kids progress in the academic stream, the rest are shifted to less academic and vocational studies with some chance of retesting. I learned with amazement that some Japanese students memorized entire encyclopedias. Japanese students at the best universities differed from those I had in Hong Kong in one big respect. Japanese students seldom attended classes, because having been accepted through arduous examinations into Tokyo University, where I taught, and **Kyoto University**, Japan's premier institutions of higher learning. They had it made for life with excellent job prospects ahead and little chance of being expelled if they passed periodic exams. When I complained to my department chairman at Tokyo University that very few students attended my lectures, he said: "You should be pleased that any attend at all; I usually have none coming to my lectures." To graduate, and almost all do, Hong Kong university students had to attend and pass courses with satisfactory grades.

Given the choice, I would rather teach Hong Kong and other Asian students than most of the 1990s students that I experienced in the U.S. before I retired, because despite the Asians' proclivity to memorize, which I could modify a bit, they applied themselves and took learning seriously—very unlike the 1990's American students. Attitude determines altitude. Except for students at America's elite universities, many professors who teach at lesser universities today lament the poor, indulgent student standards that they face. Recurring articles in the *Chronicle of Higher Education* (CHE) indicate that inattentive and unruly students have been a common feature of college teaching in the U.S. for long. One CHE article, for instance, made me frown and laugh at the same time when it reported, "Professors trade stories about chirping cell phones and rustling newspapers during lectures. They nod sympathetically at tales of freshmen snoring in the front row." Why are taxpayers unaware of such student behavior and attitudes and faculty acquiescence at public universities, which derive their budgets from how many students they enroll? Parents and their children should set their sights on the very best universities.

Clark Kerr, the late distinguished President of the University of California System and my friend, once said in jest that the chief concerns of U.S. university presidents were providing parking for the faculty, sex for the students, and winning sports for the alumni. Kerr served on the visiting boards of the Chinese University of Hong Kong, where I taught in the 1980s, and the University of Macau, where as a consultant, I founded and developed its School of Education, one of my proudest accomplishments. We also met in Berkeley. We agreed that many U.S. students were not as diligent as they used to be and inferior to students in East Asia. When he told me in the company of Mrs. Kerr that he decided to give up his Hong Kong and Macau consultations, his wife stormed, "No you won't; I don't want to give up my shopping over here!"

Gwen Ellen Morett in Suite101.com showed how teaching students with examples that are meaningful to them can help them understand:

> The Pythagorean Theorem consists of the following:
> The sum of the squares of two legs of a right triangle
> is equal to the hypotenuse squared ... The following
> consists of real life applications to introduce to
> students which can greatly ease their anxieties and
> further promote their learning ... If the teacher asks
> students how many of them play baseball or enjoy
> baseball, the majority of boys in the classroom will
> more than likely raise their hands. The teacher can
> utilize this concept by using an overhead transparency,
> chalkboard, or other advanced technological device.
> In a baseball diamond, the distance between each
> of the three bases and home plate are ninety feet

and all form right angles. If a teacher draws a line from home plate to first base, then from first base to second base and back to the home plate, the students can see a right triangle has been formed. Using the Pythagorean Theorem, the teacher can then pose the question, "How far does the second baseman have to throw the ball in order to get the runner out before he slides into the home plate? $(90)^2 + (90)^2 = c^2$, or the distance from home plate to second base. 8100 + 8100 = 16,200. The square root of 16,200 is approximately 127, so the second baseman would have to throw it about 127 feet.

My philosophy of teaching and learning is dedicated to the promotion of lifelong learning and insightful awareness. Opposed to blind regurgitation and fun-and-game activity, the best parents and teachers believe that learning and thinking are unique human potentials that can flourish through effort and insightful experience. Although I felt effective in fulfilling those aims with fifth- and sixth-graders and my own children, university teaching was something else, with course teaching schedules of several hour-long lectures a week, the poor basic skills and study habits of many U.S. students (in the 1990s, but not in 1960–70s), and other hindrances that limited proper teaching and learning. However, research, publications, and thesis students made academic life fulfilling for me.

As an elementary school teacher, I constantly thought of new lessons and supplementary aids to further my philosophy of teaching and learning, while on the half hour drive to and from Freddie Burk on the old road replaced by the I-280 today. The drive was about my only private time. Nothing intrigued me more than how I could better teach a concept with lasting effect, and nothing irritated me more than when after the fact I realized that I had missed a good opportunity. Believing that the greatest potentials of humans center in their mental powers, which cannot be fulfilled without effective programming as with a computer, I emphasized language and math adroitness and adaptability. Attention was given to some rote drilling in spelling and arithmetic, basics that must be learned through memorization and skill-building practice. However, I did my best to avoid deadening rote for its own sake. Speed games in which pupils competed on drill sheets were helpful fun. For, during those games I played loud, distracting sounds—our favorite was a recording of bell-ringing and roaring locomotives (I'm a steam locomotives fan), played while the class raced through a list of multiplication problems or a paragraph with punctuation and spelling errors. Pupils would raise their hands when they completed the sheets and I posted their names on the chalkboard for priority checking of their work. Much that the kids needed to know had to be fixed in their long-term memory with easy retrieval, as tools ready on call with know-how on how to apply them. As German philosopher Arthur Schopenhauer, wrote: "The memory should be specially taxed in youth, since it is then that it is strongest and most tenacious. But in choosing the things that should be committed to memory the utmost care and forethought must be exercised; as lessons well learnt in youth are never forgotten." With far less time with university students, I never felt satisfied with what was accomplished.

I taught the kids memorization techniques of making connections with names of people and places, etc. that they want to remember. For example, Italy is the big boot that's kicking the ball, Sicily; Britain is shaped like its currency symbol, the pound (£); Turkey is like a Thanksgiving turkey minus head and legs; and the continent of India looks like an ice cream cone. When meeting people for the first time, focus on each individual's name and connect it with something distinctive about him or her, such as his or her nose or eyes. Mnemonics can be useful, such as the name of ROY G BIV to recall the color of rainbows in order and HHSK, Hold High Singing Kings for Japan's largest ("home islands") islands in order: from north to south, Hokkaidō, Honshū (the "mainland"), Shikoku and Kyūshū. Use of phoneme-grapheme clues can be helpful. For instance, I recall Croatia by thinking "crow," the nation where my son is now stationed in the U.S. embassy. Father Matteo Ricci SJ used an elaborate memory system. Envisioning a great castle, he mentally walked through it and connected or attached words and phrases of a report or speech onto each item as he mentally walked through the castle, such as "Suffer little children" to the moat, "to come unto me" to the castle gate, and "and forbid them not" to the entry courtyard.

I dislike fun-and-games teaching that are no more than play gimmicks with little depth and follow-through for meaning and memory. Though children have fun, any learning from such teaching is superficial and helter-skelter. For example, a teacher's lesson I observed on PBS conducted an elaborate two-day pizza-making project to teach fractions. With the help of several mothers, the pupils prepared the dough on one day and baked pizzas in groups of six or so the next day. When finished, they were told to divide the pizzas evenly among group workers. If a group included six pupils, for example, each supposedly received one-sixth of the pizza. That is when fractions were supposedly to come into the picture, but the superficial reference to the arithmetic concept hardly touched the pupils' consciousness. It was obvious that eating pizza was all the kids were aware of and consumed their full attention, not fractions. Since directed teaching of fractions and their relation to other math concepts was lacking, it was a waste of time and effort. The right approach to mentoring children is to spiral them from what they already know to new concepts and expand their awareness and know-how, not to distract them.

Another example of fun-and-games teaching is attempts to expose children to other cultures through shallow song-and-dance routines. Lessons on the Chinese, Native Americans, and other ethnic groups with activities based on costumes, makeup, chopsticks, curios, singing and dancing, etc. do nothing more than create and extend stereotypes. If one could ask pupils what they learned from such lessons, they might say how much fun they were and what problems they had in baking pizzas, using chopsticks, etc.

Teachers and parents who think that children learn best when they are freed to "discover" ideas and solutions on their own with minimal, non-directed instruction should realize that research has debunked such teaching methods. As discussed in chapter three, "discovery," open-ended programs with costly textbooks and teaching aids, which have been developed and sold to many schools, have been found woefully deficient in pupil achievement when contrasted with interactive, structured programs. When the Frederic Burk principal and other teachers bought into a "discovery" math program and enthused over it,

I was skeptical. Class demonstrations were showy, and teachers and many parents thought the program matched their freewheeling, child-centered views. However, what's fun and showy can be misleading frill. Similar to the teacher who taught fractions with pizza baking, the eager scrambling of kids manipulating rods, sticks, and blocks excited my Frederic Burk colleagues. Although there was discussion after the activity, there was no or little solid follow-through with guided mentoring, drill, and memory building. I wondered how do they get addition-subtraction combinations and multiplication systematically into their long-term memory with momentary play and chatter? Youths cannot learn to read, write, and figure properly through unstructured, open-ended teaching. Elementary spelling and math must be learned and remembered, not discovered choice.

While most American parents are keenly concerned about their children's language-arts skills, especially reading, they tend to underrate the value of mathematics. Scientists regard math as the foremost "language" of thought and design. It's wrongheaded when many American parents excuse their child's poor math grades, such as saying that, "That's okay, I wasn't very good with numbers myself." As the College Board reported from the 2006 SAT results, which showed the largest drop in thirty-one years, American girls continued to do better in language, outdoing boys by eleven points. Girls continue to lag the boys in math scores, though they cut the difference from forty-two points in 2005 to twenty-six in 2006, and even more in 2009. Parents and educators excusing the girls' weaker math performance out of gender and social differences contradict the fact that Asian and European girls do as well as boys in math. This is one example of how false excuses "dumb down" the fulfillment of our children's potentials.

What follows is a sample lesson that I published in a magazine for classroom teachers. My first publication, Irene and I marveled in my being paid five cents per word ($20), so different from later publications in prestigious research journals that paid nothing, but boosted one's university career.

> New mathematics or not, one task of elementary teachers is to help children comprehend large number concepts. Numbers like *million, billion*, and *trillion* may even trouble teachers' comprehension. The difficulty is that in daily life, we do not normally face real situations wherein we handle such huge quantities of things, other than reading business and government budget news. The children can develop a "feel" for the meaning of a million by actually seeing and working with a million objects, but where can we find suitable experiences readily available that will interest them?
>
> If we are to work with a million or a billion things, we will need to learn the use of *sampling*, which in itself is an important understanding. Sampling has been overlooked in most elementary school teaching, but it is used in many fields of endeavor today. It is an important research tool. In general, we use sampling to find out something about a larger group of things. For instance, when we want to make predictions or observations about a large population of people or a quantity of aspirin pills that we could never study individually, at least easily, we can generalize with respect to the total group from the findings we obtain by studying a sample group. But we must select our sample group carefully. Oftentimes, lack of caution

in sampling techniques has caused researchers to claim more than they should. Children can begin to see the value of careful sampling as they learn how to find and handle a million or more real objects.

In order to see a million things together, a fifth-grade class that I taught decided one day to "count" the number of grass blades in a large lawn on the campus of San Francisco State College. We had previously learned the concept of *area*, the relationship of square inch to square foot, and so on, and the concept of average or arithmetic mean. In our preliminary planning, we discussed how we could estimate the total number of grass blades in the lawn under study. We decided to divide the class into two groups: one group to find the total area of the lawn, and one group to find the average number of grass blades in one square foot.

The first group of children measured the dimensions of the rectangular lawn by using long lengths of twine that they had measured into known lengths beforehand. We could have used yardsticks, but we decided it would be too tedious and time-consuming to do so. If we had had surveyor's tape measures, we would have used them. From the dimensions they found, the children multiplied the length of the lawn by its width to find the total area in square feet.

A second group of pupils used dull knives and foot rulers to cut square-inch samples of the lawn at random points, in order to get samples of lawn that were as representative as possible. Each child in this group took at least two samples back to the class in a box or bag. Seated in class, they counted and recorded the number of grass blades on each square-inch sample. The first group assisted the second group in the counting.

Pupils in the sampling group gave their reports—
the samples varied from twelve to thirty blades of
grass. We computed the arithmetic mean by adding
all of the reported blade counts and dividing by the
number of samples. The result was twenty blades.
The other group reported that the lawn's dimensions
were two hundred feet by one hundred feet, and that
the area was therefore twenty thousand square feet.

The final computation was as follows:

1. Since there are 144 square inches to one square foot,
   we multiplied 144 by twenty, the number of grass
   blades found in our sample square inches of lawn.
   This gave us 2,880 grass blades to a square foot.

2. We multiplied the figure of 2,880 by twenty thousand, the total area in square feet, and discovered
   that our lawn contained, according to our estimate
   that day, 57,600,000 grass blades! By dividing one
   million by 2,880, we found that an area of 347.2
   square feet would give us one million grass blades.
   By staking off an area of ten feet by thirty-five feet
   minus three square feet, we could see our example
   of one million objects. We could see that one billion
   grass blades, being a thousand times more than one
   million, would make a huge lawn.

Other sampling activities to gain a better
understanding of large number concepts can be
accomplished with variations of the above activity,
such as taking sample counts of small weights of
coarse sand to see how many grains of sand are
in a pound (a magnifying glass would be helpful),
counting the number of words on sample pages of
a book to get the number of words in the entire
book, and figuring how high a stack of a million

coins would stand, by measuring the height of sample stacks of twenty coins. However, I prefer the outdoors lawn activity.

Problem Pupils

Rewarding my authoritative-engaging style, the large majority of the children in my classes were lively and eager to learn. Needless to say, school children can vary greatly in background and personality. I had some pupils who appeared to lack inquisitiveness and spontaneity and were negative in every way. Expressed as depression, resentment, or smoldering anger, their contrariness was probably related to their early years, when their natural curiosity and receptivity had been hindered, perhaps through a bad illness or traumatic school or family experiences. They often found their niche as naysayers and tattletales. When such children resist and hold back, the educator should refrain from scolding and punishing. By being positive and patient, the problem kids will eventually open up if the right motivating activity is developed and rewarded. Resisters are often treated as isolates and made fun of by their classmates. What I usually did was to appoint isolates to be my "special helpers," who did chores for me, such as mixing water paints and helping to pass out papers. With responsibility to assist me and going around the room, isolates became active team players with new identities in the class.

At Windsor School, one lad, who was hardly a recluse and must have grown to be a big, strapping man, constantly interrupted lessons with mischief, outbursts, and moving about. I learned that his mother cared alone for him and two younger children, and was on relief after divorcing their no-good father. My husky sixth-grader was the "man" of the family and tested well in IQ. Experimenting, I assigned him my assistant, which gave him tacit permission to move around the classroom on his own. It worked perfectly, for being on his feet, Dan could handle his restlessness and connect with lessons. As he handled chores, Dan strolled about the classroom. At times he would revert and make a fuss, but he quickly shaped up on my glance and a finger signal. Dan attended to lessons and learned to raise his hand instead of intruding out-of-turn. Clearly respecting our relationship, he began to control himself. In my mind's eye, I can see that wide-eyed lad moving about attentively and hear his deep-throated voice contributing answers and good comments. Maybe Dan matched what Robert Brault wrote: "Conscience is less an inner ear than the memory of a mother's (teacher's) glance."

Like most teachers, I deeply regret that I have lost track of my former pupils. Never seeing them again and not knowing how their lives turned out can be hard if one delved on it too much. However, knowing can also be sad. I learned from friends that tragedy struck a fourth-grade boy I taught at Alexander Valley School whose IQ, learning readiness, and awareness outshone almost every youngster I ever taught. When I was his teacher, he presented me with a steelhead that he had caught. I do not know when, but his parents later divorced. In high school, he became a star basketball player who skipped studies for foolish recklessness. Tearing about on a motorcycle, he died in an accident at age seventeen. As they advanced through high school and maybe higher education into work, adulthood, and probable parenthood, those I have taught may not remember my name. A teacher's lot is such, which gives more reason to do the very best for their destinies while one can. Yet teachers can look forward to new classes of youngsters, unlike parents who become "unemployed" when their children leave home.

Good learners can become isolate loners when they try to outdo everyone else and are always the first to put up their hands. A chat with them usually solved the situation. I had two isolates at Windsor School whose problem was not being naysayers or overachievers, but being retarded. Going through the grades, they became class dunces. Their parents told me that the fifth-grade boys had been natural lefties who had been forced at early age to be right-handed, which may have disrupted their brain networks and created learning problems. One constantly cried and hid his head under his upraised desk cover. Although it was impossible to reverse the left-right hand problem if that was the cause of their underachievement, I tried to do something about their self-concept, class image, and learning. Assigning them as monitors to help me with chores and chatting together in lock-arm when I had recess yard duty, I also gave them remedial lessons. Once when they were absent, I spoke to their classmates about the way they treated the two isolates. I had them write down taunts they had said to the boys and had some read aloud before I asked them how they would feel if anybody said that to them. They admitted that what they did had become a harsh habit, and said other teachers hadn't tried to stop it and some even made fun of the two boys themselves. On my prompting, they pledged to reverse their viciousness and be considerate. As most realized that actions have consequences, they were fairly true to their word. While the lads improved in their learning, the biggest change was in their brightened personalities. I also prepped their next teacher, who took them under his wings as well. Teaching provides special opportunities to really affect people's lives for the better.

Learning Readiness and Awareness

Wanting the children to learn how to learn and think as a chief strategy; I sought to open their minds and senses to their bountiful, beautiful, and complex country and universe. Believing that children should develop the ability to focus their minds on whatever they are attending to, like a magnifying glass, I stressed the need to concentrate and communicate /interpret (getting and giving information) accurately. A joke I used for that idea was a telegrapher who thought the sender had misspelled "sheep" in his message and corrected it in the message. The herder unfortunately received a large shipment of sheep before his prized dog, Shep, arrived to help manage the herd. For many today, the ability to focus and feel empathy for others can be endangered by overuse of modern communication tools, as Matt Richtel (*New York Times*, June 7, 2010) wrote:

> Scientists say juggling e-mail, phone calls and other incoming information can change how people think and behave. They say our ability to focus is being undermined by bursts of information. These play to a primitive impulse to respond to immediate opportunities and threats. The stimulation provokes excitement—a *dopamine* squirt—that researchers say can be addictive. In its absence, people feel bored. The resulting distractions can have deadly consequences, as when cellphone-wielding drivers

and train engineers cause wrecks....these urges can inflict nicks and cuts on creativity and deep thought, interrupting work and family life. While many people say multitasking makes them more productive, research shows otherwise. Heavy multitaskers actually have more trouble focusing and shutting out irrelevant information, scientists say, and they experience more stress.

I taught kids that three-R skills and other curricula are absorbed most easily and become meaningful with the attitude that they are essential tools and knowledge. Although everyone would agree that humans can control their attention and thoughts, many shortchange themselves by viewing learning, reading, and thinking as undesirable chores. Inhibitions and distractions curtail many people's focus and attention span, which make it hard for them to consider anything more interesting and mentally challenging than phoning, emails, sitcoms, sports, and films.

By class demand, I usually ended the day with a game called "Simon Says," when I would give commands, such as "Simon says stand up" or "Touch your nose." By the rules of the game, they should obey commands only if they began with "Simon says." I ran a fast-paced contest, so few could escape getting caught and losing participation. That game, along with other study-related stimuli, helped to promote their focus and attention span.

It's important to realize that there are different levels of discourse and communication. I taught children to understand that we ordinarily speak with others and read newspapers at a common, everyday level. Comparing that with the U.S. Constitution, poetry, and dialogue in the Shakespeare's plays, pupils see that language, ideas, and their meanings differ in complexity. In class we enjoyed taking turns as pupil A recited a poem, such as Robert Browning's "Parting at Morning," and pupil B reacting in everyday language. A: "Round the cape of a sudden came the sea/And the sun looked over the mountain's rim." B: "Where were you, and how was the weather?" A: And straight was a path of gold for him/And the need of a world of men for me." B: "Who were your friends and were you lonely?" Since the words of the poem are commonplace, clearly A's elevated thrust differed from B's everyday tone. We recited famous lines, such as "Give me liberty or give me death!" and "And the rockets' red glare, the bombs bursting in air, gave proof through the night that our flag was still there," to fully sense meaning and see who could deliver them best. Then there are works, such as those with erudite concepts and mathematical analyses, which are impossible to understand without prior knowledge and expertise. Examples are philosophers, such as Hegel, and complex, scientific-technological works, such as Francis Crick, James Watson, and Maurice Wilkins's double helix structure of DNA and laboratory development of the swine flu vaccine.

If we count coarse, foul language beneath everyday talking and writing, then we have four levels of language complexity, starting from the lowest level: (1) vulgarity; (2) everyday dialogue; (3) profound dramatic script; and (4) the esoteric. When I returned home from the Korean War, my mother told me before I retired the first night, that tomorrow my speech would change for the better. Totally unaware that I was still speaking as a platoon sergeant, I quickly reverted to everyday dialogue. As I helped students to become aware of the different language and concept levels, mainly through science and social studies, I became gratified that they saw for themselves how important it was for them to work on level two, and somewhat with level three, before they might begin to pursue areas in level four when older. We also noted differences in everyday speech, as in respect to authority and courtesy, such as the use of "sir" and "ma'am," and "please." We had fun comparing Anglo-American differences in speaking and spelling the same language, such as pronouncing tomato: British with a hard second syllable "a" and the U.S. with a soft "a;" and in spelling: labour versus labor and al-u-min-i-um versus alu-mi-num. Lessons such as those helped to reinforce the importance of awareness and being able to read, write, and spell accurately, as well as using and understanding the great range and depth of our shared English language. Since such lessons took very little time to cover, I could wait for the right moments to interrelate them with other studies.

So that one can be aware and attend as well as possible, the three-Rs should be well-honed, embedded skills that can be easily accessed from long-term memory. Japanese samurai used the expression, "No mind," in honing all they had to know and to be capable of doing as warriors. There are no rivals to the Japanese in their dedication to the principle that training and practice makes perfect. When American players joined baseball teams in Japan, they were appalled by the hours of grueling drill that Japanese coaches regularly ran before each game. What "No mind" meant to the samurai had to be that they practiced and studied swordsmanship and combat so thoroughly that their reflexes and moves required little or no conscious thought, leaving their minds and senses free to be wary and decisive with few distractions. Keyboard typing, driving, and playing musical instruments well are excellent examples of performing basic skills without having to think about them.

Since it is human to err and constant perfection is illusory, children must realize early on that everybody makes mistakes and that mistakes found help one to improve. Awareness then includes the possibility of error on the part of others and oneself, which depending on the nature of the event, something lost or a misspelled word, people should be alert to their happening and know how to handle them. Keen awareness spots and corrects mistakes. I used to instruct my academic dean office staff that we don't have a mistake until it is too late to change it. Little has pleased me more as an educator than observing groups of pupils busily pursuing their projects, such as studying fairy shrimp with a microscope and sketching drawings, or putting their heads together to draft the latest newsletter. Scrutinizing their products and stimulating each others thinking as they worked, the children made revisions when they found room for improvement. The tremendous value of learning and sharing with others is hard to beat. I urged pupils to strive for accuracy through the habit of checking one's work and that of others, and problem solving instead of carping in recrimination. I often said that pencils have erasers for a reason, but let's not waste rubber on the same errors.

This chapter illustrated my elementary school teaching with the authoritative-engaging style of managing children, as discussed in chapters one and two. In summary, upon birth, humans are endowed with mind-body potentials that should be realized and not wasted by shortchanging childhood learning. Parents and teachers need to encourage and channel the curiosity of children and their eagerness to learn. Besides the three-R tools that must be learned and understood through meaningful practice, there are innumerable concepts, as in science and social studies, that children delight in learning if motivated to pursue them. My classroom teaching verified that children learn best when they pursue new knowledge from what they know already and see that inquiry and being informed can be enlightening and beneficial to them and others. Youth should involve preparation for lifelong learning and maximizing the chances of children for a productive, happy life.

CHAPTER FIVE

INSIGHTS FROM BIOGRAPHIC STUDIES

> It is no hard matter to get children; but after they are born, then begins the trouble, solicitude, and care rightly to train, principle, and bring them up.
>
> —Montaigne, "Of the Education of Children,"
> *Essays, 1580–88*

This chapter illustrates and extends what the previous chapters discussed by examining the lives of ten very interesting and different persons. Several others are touched on. First, careful attention is given their youthful attachment and social interaction with parents, teachers, and others to see how their learning readiness, awareness, and fundamental makeup developed in adulthood. After sketching their biographies, we compare and contrast the ten individuals by assessing their differences and similarities. Details were obtained from the autobiographies, biographies, and Internet Web sites listed at the end of this chapter.

Sandra Day O'Connor (1930-)

Justice O'Connor retired from the Supreme Court in mid-2005. She is one of the best- known Supreme Court justices in recent history and one of the most influential women in U.S. history. Many believe that O'Connor's judicial pragmatism stemmed from her youth in an isolated, ranching family. Appointed by President Ronald Reagan in 1981 and confirmed unanimously by the Senate, she was the first woman out of 108 justices to sit on the high court.

Sandra was born March 26, 1930, in El Paso, Texas. Her parents, Harry and Ada Mae Day, owned the Lazy-B-Cattle Ranch in southeastern Arizona, where she had a hard, but happy childhood. The ranch ("lots of land but little water") did not have electricity or running water until she was seven. Water for the ranch came from thirty-five windmills and wells, which demanded constant oiling and maintenance to keep them going. Since their closest neighbors lived twenty-five miles away, the family spent their days mostly in isolation, and went into town once a week to get provisions and pick up mail. Sandra spent many years as an only child, the family's center of attention, as her younger brother and sister were not born until she was eight. She befriended the cowboys and kept pets, including a bobcat and a hawk, and was an avid reader. Riding horses when she was six, Sandra has written a children's book about her beloved pony, Chico, and her memories of rattlesnakes, thunderstorms, and desert beauty. Active in ranch work, she was an unspoiled tomboy, close to her hands-on dad. She wrote that her mother "was a tidy package of good looks, competence, and charm" (page 49, 2003), which is praise, but seems less than intimate. Sandra said that brother Alan was her mother's favorite, not her.

She didn't shy away and stay homebound as many girls might have, but she knew her limitations. Relating the urgency and difficulties of repairing a failed wellhead, Sandra wrote,

> It took strength, time, skill, and energy to repair. There was little I could do to help. The work required more strength that I had. I could serve like an operating-room nurse—I would get a wrench, a hammer, or another tool that was needed and put it into my father's outstretched hand. More often, I read a book I had brought along or I watched the work and engaged in desultory conversation with the men" (O'Connor, 2003, page 3).

The ranch's isolation limited home studies and prevented formal education with others, so Sandra's parents sent her to live with her maternal grandmother in El Paso. She attended Radford School, a private academy for girls, from kindergarten through high school, where she had excellent teachers and schoolmates. Homesick, she returned to the ranch for a year before graduating with good marks at the age of sixteen. Sandra credits much of her later success to her grandmother, whose loving influence motivated her to strive and fulfill her potentials. It is clear that Sandra's parents and grandmother were authoritative-engaging caregivers.

After Radford, Sandra attended Stanford University, where she enrolled at Stanford Law School after receiving her BA degree in economics, magna cum laude in

1950. Completing her law degree in two years instead of the normal three, she served on the *Stanford Law Review* and received membership in the Order of the Coif, a legal honor society. Graduating third out of a class of 102, Sandra met her future husband, John Jay O'Connor III, a fellow law student. They had three sons. She has often praised Stanford, it's enriching environs, professors, and students, for stimulating her thinking and opening her mind to the world.

Despite gender discrimination, Sandra was not without work. She was deputy attorney general in San Mateo, California (1952–53), which she said "influenced the balance of my life because it demonstrated how much I did enjoy public service." After a stint as a civilian attorney for the military while John was an Army lawyer in Germany (1954–57), she practiced law in Arizona and became a state assistant attorney general (1965–69). She was then appointed to the state senate and reelected twice, winning the majority leader seat in 1973—the first woman to hold that post. After election to a county judgeship (1975), she was appointed to the Arizona Court of Appeals in 1979, where she worked until her appointment to the U.S. Supreme Court in 1981. Her book, *Majority of the Law*, discusses the rise of females in the legal profession among other themes, and how different it is today than when she first practiced law and law firms refused to employ her. When Ruth Bader Ginsburg was nominated to the Court by President Clinton in 1993 and confirmed, O'Connor wept with joy. As she has often said and apparently abided by, "Society as a whole benefits immeasurably from a climate in which all persons, regardless of race or gender, may have the opportunity to earn respect, responsibility, advancement and remuneration based on ability."

John Fitzgerald Kennedy (1917–1963)

Born to Joseph and Rose Kennedy in Brookline, Massachusetts, JFK, America's beloved thirty-fifth president, was assassinated forty-six years later near the end of his third year in the White House. Led by his father's strong-willed paternalism and ever-driving energy, the family sought to be identified as outstanding Americans in opposition to bigotry and snobbery towards the Irish and Catholics. Craving status and power, Joseph forged great wealth in real estate and stock market speculation, bootlegging during Prohibition, distribution of movies, and becoming the leading distributor of choice British liquors in the U.S. after the repeal of Prohibition. Exclusive clubs that refused him membership padded his wealth by buying his booze. As he thundered in typical tone: "Those narrow-minded bigoted sons of bitches barred me because I was an Irish Catholic and son of a barkeep. You can go to Harvard (as he and his sons did) and it doesn't mean a damned thing. The only thing these people understand is money." However, Joe's political donations and restless lobbying earned him recognition and high-profile appointments, such as Ambassador to Britain (1938–1940). Disputing President Franklin Roosevelt's support of Britain's fight against Germany, his anti-Semitism and arguments to appease Hitler brought about his resignation.

Demanding and cajoling his children to be doers, winners, and fast thinkers, Joseph went to great lengths to do what he believed essential for them, especially if it could be bought. He groomed Joseph Jr., his oldest, to be a future president, but Jr. died in a tricky bombing run that he piloted across the channel. Senior turned his aspirations onto his second son, Jack, who was bookish and sickly with a weak back, and had always been a runner-up against Joe's athleticism and popularity. Jack had his own mind, but somehow complied with his father's wishes, even to end a serious romance with Ingra Arvad, a "luscious" woman separated from her husband, which lasted three years into Jack's Navy service. Ingra is said to have agreed to the breakup after receiving a generous sum of money from Joseph, who had been monitoring the affair through wiretaps and informers. Jack's painful back and ulcer, which he endured through his naval career, including his heroism in the PT-109 saga, reflected his fierce determination and energy, a common characteristic of the Kennedy children.

Mother of the family's four sons and five girls, Rose Kennedy was subservient to Joseph, even after she learned of his adultery with Hollywood actresses, particularly Gloria Swanson. Fervently Catholic, Rose would leave her children to servants for long religious retreats and European trips. Her girls were educated at the Noroton Convent Boarding School, run by the Sisters of the Sacred Heart and the order's convents in Europe. Rose herself had been educated by Sacred Heart nuns in Boston. Relations with her many children were sober and detached, often through written instructions. Instead of managing her brood with sensitive and affectionate mindfulness, she oversaw them as a somber, remote overlord. Unlike

Joseph, she never visited Jack during his difficult prep school years.

According to his biographers, Kennedy was a "prisoner of sex" with an insatiable craze that he satisfied with diverse, willing women, including showgirls, stewardesses, socialites, campaign workers, and even actress Marilyn Monroe. Edward Klein wrote, "That John Kennedy felt compelled to have casual sex under his wife's nose says a good deal about how completely his ego was defined by the seduction of women." Klein also wrote that according to psychoanalyst Sue Erikson Bloland, "Kennedy himself gave us a clue to his pathological behavior when he complained that his mother was cold and distant and never hugged him or showed him any affection. His compulsive womanizing can be seen as the desperate effort of a deeply wounded child to obtain what was missing from his seemingly glamorous life—the experience of a genuinely intimate connection" (page 168). Jack often did not know his liaisons' names nor cared, calling them "sweetie" or "kiddo" the next morning. His womanizing is well-known today, but it appears not to have disrupted his work as president and has not diminished admiration for him. Those of us who are old enough can recall where we were when we learned of his tragic death. I was teaching a class at San Francisco State and all of us broke down into tears and remorse with the shocking news.

Helping us to understand Kennedy's psyche, Klein also wrote:

> It is generally accepted as a fact by historians that Rose was an absentee mother. What is perhaps less understood is the confusion that Rose sowed in her children's emotional lives. On the one hand, she

insisted on outward displays of family solidarity; on the other, she did not permit expression of such anxieties privately, within the confines of their own home. Inevitably, her contradictory behavior left its mark on Jack Kennedy (pages 169–170).

As Chafe wrote, "The Kennedy home, therefore, was a household of many demands, enormous contradictions, and oftentimes very little affection or emotional support. Joe was the dominant presence, injecting competition into every aspect of family life" (page 100). Hamilton's biography says that Jack's decision to resist his father's stand against FDR's aid to Britain was Jack's crucial intellectual and political break from his dad.

Besides pressuring Jack and the others to study hard and learn, Joe challenged them at dinner with provocative questions and outrageous remarks. The father's governing manner with his children meant that he made strong use of his persuasive, negotiating skills to guide what he believed to be their best interests and potential greatness, especially in public service. To get his way, Joseph did not just dictate. He took time to argue alternate courses of action with his kids and when necessary, he bargained bribes and sought support and favors from notables. Using this book's discussion of different styles of raising children, he was perhaps 30 percent authoritative and 70 percent dictatorial. Therefore, although they often disagreed with their father, the Kennedy children adhered to his wishes because they knew that he loved them and cared for their welfare and success. The difference between a tyrant and a paternalist is that the former rules absolutely with little feeling for and consideration of others, while the latter benevolently supplies needs to those under his wings and controls them as he or she believes is beneficial for them. Published soon after his death in 2009, *True Compass: A Memoir* by Ted Kennedy, the youngest of the brood, verifies the father's devotion to his nine children. It appears that Joseph treated Ted with greater tenderness than Jack and other siblings, a common parental trait for the youngest. Ted also told of the competitive spirit and commitment to public service that his "Dad" instilled in the brood.

Compared to Jack Kennedy's privileged childhood and mercurial, short life, Sandra Day O'Connor's life was pastoral and integrated. It is interesting that while psychologists realize that childhoods vary greatly to produce differing personalities and behavior patterns, the public generally assumes that people are more alike than different. Although most people are aware of their own inner and situational complexities, they view others through naïve lens, such as their appearance, profession, and what brand of auto they drive. In reality, what they perceive is just the surface—the tip of the iceberg—and that we usually assume more understanding of others than is warranted, as the next case history demonstrates. Before we close on JFK's upbringing and early life, his later life as a successful politician and popular president show that in most ways, he matured far beyond his father's domination.

Robert Philip Hanssen (1944-)

Born in Chicago, Robert was Howard and Vivian Hanssen's only child. On February 18, 2001, FBI agents arrested Robert for selling secrets to the Soviets. A good student through high school, but one who always carried a chip on his shoulder and seldom did more than what was minimally required, Bob dropped out of Northwestern University's dental school because he disliked its curriculum—"too much spit." He transferred to Northwestern's Business School where he completed a MBA degree in accounting and information systems in 1971. A leading accounting firm, Touche Ross & Co., hired him as a junior auditor, a choice job offering a bright future.

However, Bob's inner needs for thrill and power caused him to drop accounting and join the Chicago Police Department as a rookie cop when he earned far less. Wanting his son to be a doctor or dentist, his policeman father denounced Bob's decision as disgusting and stupid. Soon, because of Chicago's rampant police corruption and the department's need for undercover agents unknown to older police, he was one of the greenhorn cops who were enlisted to be covert agents. Hanssen proved to be exceptionally sharp in tracking down crooked cops. Eventually, he won choice assignment to the elite intelligence unit, where he happily immersed himself in quantities of dossiers and confidential material. The unit's head, Jack Clarke, said Bob was a good agent, but he felt that Bob manipulated him and others, acting as if he was smarter than all of them. In 1976, Hanssen joined the FBI and worked close to retirement as an agent before his conviction in 2001 as "the most damaging FBI agent in U.S. history."

Robert Hanssen and his wife, Bonnie, were devout members of the ultra-conservative and anti- Communist Opus Dei Catholic society, which became widely known through Dan Brown's sensational novel of 2003. The Hanssen's loathed Bill and Hillary Clinton. With three sons and three daughters, aged fifteen to thirty in 2001, the family was viewed by their neighbors as being social and friendly. But they saw Bob as a cordial, but highly confirmed loner and impossible to get close to. At FBI social gatherings, he ignored his colleagues and stood apart from others. He spoke in a hard-to-hear voice and wore thick eyeglasses for bad nearsightedness. Everyone viewed Bonnie as extremely attractive with a lovely figure; a "knockout" when she entered a room. The two seemed to raise their children with affectionate care. Religious faith, bedtime stories, soccer, good school grades, dinner table conversation when Bob could take teasing over his computer gadgets, etc., all of that gave the impression that the Hanssen family was normal.

At work, however, Bob felt shunned and much lower-ranked than he deserved. Like Jack Clarke in Chicago, his FBI colleagues recognized his expertise in computers, but they disliked him as rigid, cunning, and an antisocial misfit, whose every action seemed arrogant. They tired of his perpetual scowl and ranting about the Communists, though, of course, they also opposed the Reds. Lifelong Catholics among them resented the convert's proselytizing of Opus Dei. In 1979, Bob offered secrets to the Soviets for money as well, as to show he could get away with it, get even with the FBI, and offset what he saw as a dead-end life. His first betrayal identified a Russian intelligence general who sold information to the FBI, for which Bob was paid $20,000. After twenty-two years and $1.43 million in cash and goods paid him by the Russians, he was sentenced to life imprisonment, and the FBI suffered a scandal of immense proportions. When arrested, he said sarcastically, "What took you so long?"

The above came from Elaine Shannon and Ann Blackman's book, which reported that Howard, Bob's father, was "a harsh taskmaster (and) extremely strict" with his son; but their book lacks further details pertinent to this chapter, especially Bob's relationship with his mother. Lawrence Schiller's book tells more about how Howard ruled the household as a virtual tyrant. A cop in Chicago for almost thirty years and lieutenant of an anti-Communist unit his last eleven years before he retired to Florida in 1972, Howard raised Robert as he might have run a boot camp for the worst juvenile offenders. Her timid protests falling on deaf ears, Vivian offered very little sanctuary for her son. Alone with Bob, Vivian undoubtedly commiserated with him, but she sustained Howard's harshness by saying that he had to be obeyed. A tyrannical father and weak, cowering mother can make for a dangerous combination for children, as we shall also see with Adolf Hitler.

Tyrants who demand the impossible can produce inner if not open resentment in those under their sway. As he demeaned and abused Bob, Howard commanded the boy to be the very best in whatever he did. Such contradictory upbringing explains Bob's arrogant demeanor and his off-and-on work characteristics of being lazy or lost in his thoughts, and at times brilliant. Speculation into his relation with his mother and attitude towards women can be gleaned from the ways he handled his obsession with sex. Robert enjoyed taking photographs of his wife, Bonnie, in sexy poses and even their having sex, which he boastfully showed to an old friend. Also, violating common sense and security rules by using his real name and his own PC and e-mail address, he e-mailed photos and descriptions of his wife and their relations to a sex Web site. Also, though a religious devotee who attended mass each morning, Bob frequented a strip club and consorted with an exotic dancer, whom he gave a secondhand, luxury auto, a credit card to pay for the auto's maintenance, and a laptop computer that he had programmed with a secret code that she could never open. His excesses finally turned the poor woman into a drug addict and prostitute. Bob's emotional problems and betrayal can be traced to his childhood.

Interviewing Vivian, aged eighty-eight, shortly after her son's arrest, Lawrence Schiller learned about the birthday party that she had arranged for six-year-old Bob with lively children and their mothers in attendance. Bob sat immobile in his chair. Entering the scene, Howard immediately started to tease Bob. Learning that his blindfolded son had pinned the tail on the wall donkey's face, Howard said,

> "Right in the kisser, eh? Tell you what, Bob. I guess you don't know doo-doo from spit!" All the kids roared with laughter. Tears came into Bob's eyes, and into his mother's as well. Reflexively Vivian lifted her hand from Bob's shoulder...after the party was over, Howard brought Bob back into the room where the paper donkey was still tacked to the wall. "When you get into a contest," the father said, "win!"

That's it. Don't coast on mother love, boy. There's a tough, ugly, double-crossing world outside, and the only way to beat it is to win.' He spoke as if Bob were on the verge of manhood.

After more admonishment, Howard tried to get Bob to pin the tail on the donkey's rear end by whirling him around the room by his feet before each attempt, which of course the boy failed to do. "Robert was screaming. 'Daddy, stop it! Please stop it! Please stop it!' Vivian stood in the next room, bent over the kitchen sink. She was weeping, silently." After the father whirled the boy over and over again, Bob threw up on the floor. Howard forced Bob's face into the vomit, as if he was "a cheap punk" in the station's interrogation room, and said, "I did this, because I want you to know how bad it feels when you lose. This is how it feels, Robert. Got it?" Vivian came in timidly from the kitchen. She was trembling. "You can't do what you're doing to the boy," she managed to say. "He's delicate." Her voice pinched off when she saw the look in her husband's eye ... And she cowered away.

Adolf Hitler (1889–1945)

Providing insight into the development of his character, Hitler's family background is bizarre. Born out of wedlock, Adolf's father was named Alois Schicklgruber, the surname being that of his mother. When his father, a wandering miller with the name of Johann George Hiedler, finally legitimized Alois' birth twenty-five years later, Alois changed his surname from Schicklgruber to Hitler. During World War II, American GIs ridiculed Adolf Hitler by calling him variations of Schicklgruber. Adolf's mother, Klara, was twenty-five when she married Alois, aged forty-eight, who had had two wives prior. Alois and Klara knew each other well, as they were second cousins, and Klara had lived with Alois and his second wife for years as a foster daughter, which underlines their difference in age. Their first child's birth came four months came after they married. Born in 1889, Adolf was the third of six children born to Klara.

The Hitler household also included two children born of Alois' second wife, who was Irish; the first wife did not have children. One was Alois Jr., Adolf's half-brother, who became a jailed thief and bigamist and deserted his family in England. Alois Jr.'s son, William Patrick Hitler, tried to blackmail the Führer on the rumor that his paternal great-grandfather was Jewish. William also lectured about his uncle in the U.S., and then joined the U.S. Navy. As Adolf's political power gained strength in the 1920s, he whitewashed his family's mishmash genealogy and quashed opponents' rumors, especially the possibility of his having Jewish blood. Adamant that the Germans were a master race, which justified oppression of others, Hitler's obsession with eugenics and his belief in a pure Aryan bloodline flew in the face of his family's legacy.

Starting in 1928, half-sister Angela served Hitler as his Berchtesgaden housekeeper until 1936, when she left to marry a professor of architecture. Hitler so disliked her loss because of her fine pastries and desserts that he refused to send a wedding present. Angela and her daughter, Angelika (Geli) Raubal, were the only kinfolk whom Hitler stayed in contact with, probably because, as Shirer wrote, Geli was the "only truly deep love" of Hitler's life (page 10). Rebelling against Hitler's domination of her every move, Geli committed suicide in 1931 (Shirer, page 132).

Alois disciplined young Adolf with daily beatings, as common then by fathers in Austria and Germany, but probably not with Alois' mean spirit. He demanded that Adolf succeed in school so he could enter the civil service as he had, but the boy insisted on becoming an artist.

> The story of the bitter, unrelenting struggle of the boy, not yet in his teens, against a hardened and, as he said, domineering father is one of the few biographical items which Hitler sets down in great detail and with apparent sincerity and truth in *Mein Kampf...* "Artist! No! Never as long as I live!"... My father would never depart from his "Never!" And I intensified my "Nevertheless!" (Shirer, page 11).

Instead of yielding as other Austrian and German boys to their fathers, Adolf mounted a "fierce, unbending will," and retaliated by refusing to study and do well at school.

In the father's absence, his mother showered him with sweets and attention, favoring him over the other children. Showing that he loved his mother, Hitler always carried her photo. As Führer, who cold-bloodedly ordered the slaughter of eleven million people, six million of them Jews, he, however, ordered compensation given to the Jewish doctor who had attended to his mother, who died of breast cancer in 1907. A secondary school dropout, Hitler never completed his education and the would-be artist failed to gain admission to art academies. Coetzee wrote that for two years the school dropout lazed at home reading westerns and dabbling with drawings and the piano. He and his mother lived off of the departed father's pension. Joining the army in World War I, he was awarded two Iron Crosses for bravery and being a reliable message carrier, which typically earned higher promotion than his rank of corporal. His mates viewed him as peculiar. After World War I, Adolf Hitler wandered about with little means before he grasped leadership of the fledging Nazi Party in 1921 through his charismatic, patriotic speechmaking.

As Germany's absolute dictator in World War II, Hitler's thinking and actions perfectly characterized the authoritarian mind. As John Keegan wrote in his analysis of the Führer's leadership style, hundreds of miles from the fronts safe in his many headquarters, Hitler dictated battle decisions down to minor units and how they should be armed. Professing impeccable expertise, he constantly overruled and ridiculed his generals, many of whom committed suicide and suffered mental breakdowns, death sentences, and imprisonment. Typical of authoritarians, instead of blaming himself for Germany's looming defeat, he "ranted that, if the war were lost, it would be because the German people had not been worthy of him" (page 310).

Minimizing any decency that he may have gained from his mother and maximizing fierce, indignant self-righteousness in conflict with his father, his personality manifested crafty opportunism, inhumanity, and explosive nationalism. Psychologically, Hitler resolved his conflicted parental attachments by rationalizing that he embodied a god-like genius, awaiting recognition and opportunity. With similar psychopathy, Joseph Stalin slaughtered even more victims than Hitler. Psychiatrist Karl Menninger wrote, "What's done to children, they will do to society." It is astounding that an uneducated person from lower-class, peasant stock with psychopathic mentality like Adolf Hitler's could possibly become dictator of a nation so steeped in aristocratic and cultural traditions.

The Trapp Family

Maria Augusta Trapp dedicated her life to God and Church to become a nun at the Benedictine convent of Nonnberg, Austria. While still on probation, she reluctantly obeyed her Mother Abbess to go to the nearby villa of Baron Georg von Trapp, retired captain in Austria's Navy and a widower. His baronetcy came by way of his heroic service as a World War I submarine commander. Appointed at first to teach Maria, a bedridden girl, in swift succession the would-be nun became governess for the baron's seven children, the housekeeper-in-charge, and finally the children's stepmother as baroness.

After Maria was born in 1905, Maria's mother died of pneumonia two years later. Often traveling, her father deposited the baby with an elderly uncle and his spouse, who raised Maria with discipline and atheist, socialist views. The family's only child, she grew up very lonely. While studying to be a teacher, Maria had a remarkable religious awakening, which led to her decision to become a postulant at the Nonnberg Abbey in 1924. Once there, she was often scolded for behavior that was considered unbecoming to a nun, such as running and speaking freely, which she said stemmed from her past mountain climbing and sports activities and upbringing. Her poor health led to a doctor's recommendation that she needed outdoor activity and her eventual assignment to the Trapp villa.

Reporting to Baron Georg von Trapp, he informed Maria that "you are the twenty-sixth in a long line of nurses, governesses, and teachers we have had to look after them since their poor mother died four years ago...The last teacher stayed with us only two months, but I have the feeling it will be different this time." The five girls and two boys found Maria to their liking, because contrary to her predecessors, she managed them with little formality, and won them over with her warmth and bubbling activities. Attending to them with her authoritative-engaging manner, willingness to admit her own mix-ups, and holding nothing back, including anger, she endeared herself to the children as one who was, not only sincerely interested in each of them, but was forthright as well.

In time, Maria modified Baron von Trapp's aristocratic policies on decorum, such as no sports other than croquet and walking. They had no play clothes and shoes. Music and singing became the mainstay of Maria's binding attachment with her charges. With her guitar and a rich repertoire of songs that she had learned while touring the countryside, she taught the oldest girl to play the guitar and gathered the children around her to sing, seated comfortably by the inviting fireplace. When the father returned home for Christmas, he found his brood sitting on the carpet, instead of dignified on chairs and sofa. When Maria apologized for the impropriety, von Trapp surprisingly put her at ease and happily joined the caroling with his violin. With her introduction of the Advent wreath, candle, and music, the family enjoyed Christmas as they never had before. Just as Maria...

was about to leave the house for Midnight Mass, the
Captain (what she called von Trapp) had come out
of his room and, taking my hand in both of his, had
said, "I always feared Christmas more than any other
day. But this year, you have made it very beautiful
for us. Thank you." There was a warm light in the
beautiful, dark eyes which, for the first time since
I had known him, did not look pained and restless.
(page 47).

More changes also brightened the household.

In 1927, about a year after she went to the von Trapp
villa, Georg and Maria married. However, Maria did not
marry Georg von Trapp because she was in love with him.
As Joan Gearin wrote,

> She fell in love with the children at first sight, but
> not their father. When he asked her to marry him,
> she was not sure if she should abandon her religious
> calling but was advised by the nuns to do God's
> will and marry Georg. "I really and truly was not
> in love. I liked him but didn't love him. However,
> I loved the children, so in a way I really married the
> children…by and by I learned to love him more
> than I have ever loved before or after."

After financial losses during the Depression and the rise
of Nazism, which Georg refused to honor, the Trapp family emigrated to the U.S. in 1939 and supported themselves
with singing appearances, which they had begun in Austria, winning first place in the Salzburg Music Festival in
1936. In Europe and America, their singing of Renaissance
and baroque music, madrigals, and folk songs received
much acclaim. A farm in Stowe, Vermont became their
American home, which they named Cor Unum, from

descriptions of how the first Christians lived in Jerusalem in Acts of the Apostles,

> "cor unum et anima una," "They were one heart and one soul." Maria wrote that love is the most important element in life: "…we see more and more that only one thing is necessary to be happy and to make others happy, and that one thing is not money, nor connections, nor health—it is love" (Trapp, page 311).

Richard Rodgers and Oscar Hammerstein converted Maria's autobiography into *The Sound of Music*, a musical that opened on Broadway on November 16, 1959, starring Mary Martin as Maria. It ran for 1,443 performances, an overwhelming popular success. Hollywood produced a movie version of the musical in 1965 with Julie Andrews as Maria, which became a beloved film.

Information is scarce about Maria's childhood and family relations. What's known is that her pre-convent atheist and socialist views came from her guardians, and she enjoyed outdoor and sports activities, which included trekking about the Alps and its villages. Although it is said that her uncle's household was strict, the young girl must have had positive attachment with her guardians and received sufficient education and awareness to go to college to become a teacher. Maria's sudden conversion completely reversed her anti-religious views and led to her decision to become a nun. Embracing religion as she did, Maria had to have been searching for greater meaning and purpose in life. However, unsuited to the sober, constricted life of the convent, she found happiness and purpose with Georg and the Trapp family.

Henry James Jr. (1843–1916)

A prominent American writer and intellectual born in New York City, Henry James authored 20 novels, 112 stories, 12 plays, and many literary essays. Required study in literature courses, his most famous works include *Daisy Miller* (1879), a novel about an innocent, young lady whose American ways and values conflict with European sophistication, and *The Turn of the Screw* (1898), a complex, ghost tale that Benjamin Britten converted into an opera (1954). It has also been made into many movies, such as "The Innocents," starring Deborah Kerr in 1961. Works by James focused on internal, psychological turmoil and conflicts between imaginative protagonists and their troubling situations. His older brother by little more than a year, William, became a famous psychology professor at Harvard. In my undergraduate course on classic novels, the professor said that while William wrote like a novelist, his brother, Henry, wrote like a psychologist.

Very well-off with inherited wealth, the family with four boys and one girl often traveled to Europe for long stays. Seemingly more at home in Britain and France than America, they dwelled on cherished aesthetic and religious touchstones. Several of Junior's novels grew out of his critical observations of Americans in Europe. Having lived in England for long periods, he renounced his U.S. citizenship to become a British citizen in 1916 in protest to America's reluctance to aid Britain in World War I. By way of lectures, essays in literary magazines, and many self-published books, his father, Henry James Sr., was well-known in intellectual circles of mid-nineteeth century America. His friends included Emerson, Hawthorne, and Thoreau. Minus a leg from a horrible fire accident in youth, James Sr.'s recuperation sparked his belief that humanity could perfect itself and bring about heaven on earth through a "regenerative process of man—from awakening, purgation, illumination—and that a new birth for man was the secret of Divine Creation and Providence" (Edel, page 8). Free to journey, ponder, write, and attend to his family, Senior found inspiration in his wife, Mary, who reciprocated his deep affection. They treasured their children, shared appreciation for ideas, and were friends of the great minds of their time.

As biographer Leon Edel also wrote, James Sr. fell in love with Mary Walsh when they first met. Mary and younger sister Catherine sat entranced in their parlor listening "to the strange and vivid eloquence of the young Albany scion, as he expounded his unorthodox religious views; both girls were charmed and spellbound" (p. 10). James and Mary married in 1840. As if she was wife number two, Catherine became a family member and the brood's second mother. Having servants like the Kennedy family, but quite unlike the distant and often absent Rose, Mary was as Junior described her—"all-saving service and trust." "Mary James seems to have governed with a certain grace and a quiet unperturbed dignity. Her domain was, however, far from quiet" (page 12), as the boys as teens constantly challenged each other in debate. Senior served as moderator, and Mary tried to conciliate. As the mother sought peace and agreement, she was "something strong-yet-yielding, firm-yet-soft," serving all sides of arguments, first this and then the other. Junior sized up family interaction by saying, "we wholesomely breathed inconsistency and ate and drank contradictions."

With parent-child attachments positively set emotionally and intellectually, the family circle was obviously a challenging, engaging environment in which brains and wits mattered, along with keen learning readiness and awareness. As Ebel described Junior's idyllic, secure youth, "The childhood of Henry James was spacious in home and in city, a world rich and various, wrapped in outward security and 'floating in such a clean light social order'" (page 28). Junior "came to be his mother's favorite son. He was called 'angel'" (page 19).

Lending further insight into the James family, Gary Wills wrote that, "Life among the Jameses was a perpetual tussle for control. Partly because there was so much unconventionality and gleeful disorder in the family, control was a strategy and a goal for most of the members." Richardson, William's biographer (page 38) said that members of the James family applied their own special methods to gain control—

> William found ways to use his neurasthenia and precarious health to get his way. Henry Junior became famous for his control with his language, his point of view, his life, and his papers, characterizing James Sr. as a "crackpot," who "flitted from Calvinism to Transcendentalism to Swedenborgianism to Fourierism to Free Love," writing "unwanted and unread" books about them all.

Wills said that, "His children were able, in time, to mock (mainly kindly) this Dickensian character, but not to break free of his influence. They had lived too long under the Niagara Falls of his enthusiasms. Henry, the novelist, was drawn to séances, ghosts, electrical shock treatment, and health fads."

Junior never married, and those close to him saw him as feminine. Ebel elaborates on his suspected homosexuality. Whether any of that came from his mother's tender indulgence is there to consider, especially in contrast to JFK's womanizing that many say grew out of his mother's cold detachment. Junior had to have been influenced by having a father whose disability and commitment to intellectualizing offset sports and outdoor activities. Henry Jr.'s rival and soul mate was his brother William, who seemed to best him in everything and enjoyed privileges of being the oldest son, like going to the theater and about with the parents while the younger kids stayed home. Yet, as it was with JFK's relationship with his older brother, Joseph, the brothers were thoroughly devoted to each other.

Psychologists have studied siblings' birth order and produced controversial conclusions about the influence of birth order on children's behavior. For example, the first child, like William, whether male or female, is said to be serious-minded and studious, which agrees with the fact that first-borns tend to be teachers and intellectuals. It has also been said that second sons, like Henry, tend to be emotional and extroverted, and second daughters are creative and introverted.

Sir Winston Spencer Churchill (1874–1965)

Churchill is best known in the U.S. as Britain's legendary prime minister during World War II. His father, Randolph Churchill, was the third son of the seventh Duke of

Marlborough and held high government offices, such as Chancellor of the Exchequer (equivalent to, but has more authority than the U.S. Secretary of the Treasury). Known for his fiery wit and uninhibited insolence, Randolph added to his ancestors' besmeared history of extravagance and immorality, and died of syphilis in 1895. He and Jennie Jerome, a New York debutante, decided to marry three days after they first met. Jennie's father, Leonard Jerome, was a multimillionaire, horse racing father, who went on hunting expeditions with Buffalo Bill Cody. Randolph and Jennie married a year later in 1874 after the seventh duke's haggling with Jennie's father over the dowry, which finalized on $3 million in today's values. Beautiful, witty, and a tolerable pianist, Jennie charmed her way through numerous suitors. It is rumored that Winston's brother, Jack, had a different father. At age forty-six, Lady Randolph married a twenty-six-year-old Scots-Guard junior officer, who was only one year older than Winston. Although she spent little time with him, Winston admired his mother. He wrote of his memory of her, "My mother always seemed to me a fairy princess: a radiant being possessed of limitless riches and power. She shone for me like the Evening Star. I loved her dearly—but at a distance" (Randolph Churchill, page 35).

Winston's parents sent him to boarding schools; the first was St. George School, known for its harsh discipline, just before his seventh birthday. Parents from afar, Jennie never visited her son at school and Randolph thought poorly of him, believing him to be a pathetic never-to-do-well. Winston could recall only one dinner with his father when they drank and conversed at length. Despite his loneliness and sadness at school, he remained sincerely affectionate toward his parents, as his many letters to them testify, typically begging to see them. When he finished the cavalry course at the Royal Military Academy of Sandhurst in 1894, which he began at age twenty, Jennie helped to advance his career by pulling strings with her many powerful friends.

With such parents, most fortunately for him and the free world, Winston had a dedicated and loving nanny in Elizabeth Anne Everest, who provided the warm attachment and nurturance every child should have. Her managing style was clearly authoritative-engaging. Employed about a month after Winston's birth, Mrs. Everest (unmarried; female housekeepers were called Mrs.) attended to him and brother Jack in Kent County until they reached adolescence. Picking up her bias for Kent, Churchill purchased Chartwell there in 1922. Jenkins wrote, "She was the central emotional prop of Winston's childhood" and that she had "among other attributes great descriptive power" (pages 9 and 10). After her service as nanny ended, Mrs. Everest and the boys stayed in touch through correspondence and visits. She would write to Winston, "My darling Winny" and "Lots of love and kisses Fm your loving old woom." He wrote, "My darling Old Woom" and "Good Bye darling, I hope you will enjoy yourself, with love from Winny."

Winston's son, Randolph, wrote, "Mrs. Everest was not only the friend and companion of his (Winston's) youth, schooldays and early manhood; she remained warmly cherished in his memory throughout his life" (page 34). Winston and his brother, Jack, rushed to Mrs. Everest's bedside on word of her imminent passing, Winston wrote to his mother the same day his beloved nanny died,

> Everything that could be done—was done. I engaged
> a nurse, but she only arrived for the end. It was very
> sad & her death was shocking to see—but I do not
> think she suffered much pain. She was delighted to
> see me on Monday and I think my coming made her
> die happy…I shall never know such a friend again.
> (Randolph Churchill, page 245)

In his one and only novel, *Savrola*, written four years
after Mrs. Everest's death, Winston touched on the main
character's nanny, who had "nursed him from his birth up
with a devotion and care which knew no break." He then
philosophized on such "love of a foster-mother for her
charge appears absolutely irrational. It is one of the few
proofs, not to be explained by the association of ideas, that
the nature of mankind is superior to mere utilitarianism,
and that his destinies are high" (Randolph Churchill, page
34). The only photo by his bed when Winston died was
of Everest. Out of devotion to duty, teachers, nurses, and
others who do all that they can for those in their care help
to define humane commitment.

Since it is well-known that the boy did poorly as a student and was only accepted into Sandhurst Royal Military
Academy after his third attempt following a crash course,
we can assume that his nanny and governess did not
enhance the boys' learning readiness much. Churchill's
description of his youthful education at home underlines
the problems that come from poor teacher-pupil relations
and the failure to teach pupils at their ability level:

> It was at 'The Little Lodge' I was first menaced with
> Education. The approach of a sinister figure described
> as 'the Governess' was announced. Her arrival was
> fixed for a certain day. In order to prepare for this

day Mrs. Everest produced a book called *Reading without Tears*. It certainly did not justify its title in my case. I was made aware that before the Governess arrived I must be able to read without tears. We toiled each day. My nurse pointed with a pen at the different letters. I thought it all very tiresome...We continued to toil every day, not only at letters but at words, and also at what was much worse, figures. Letters after all had only got to be known, and when they stood together in a certain way one recognized their formation and that it meant a certain sound or wore which one uttered when pressed sufficiently. But the figures were tied into all sorts of tangles and did things to one another, which it was extremely difficult to forecast with complete accuracy. You had to say what they did each time they were tied up together, and the Governess apparently attached enormous importance to the answer being exact. If it was not right, it was wrong. It was not any use being 'nearly right.' In some cases these figures got into debt with one another: you had to borrow one or carry one, and after-wards you had to pay back the one you had borrowed...They became a general worry and preoccupation. More especially was this true when we descended into a dismal bog called 'sums.' There appeared to be no limit to these. When one sum was done, there was always another. Just as soon as I managed to tackle a particular class of these afflictions, some other much more variegated type was thrust upon me. My mother took no part in these impositions, but she gave me to understand that she approved of them and she sided with the Governess almost always (1930, pages 1–2).

Yet, Churchill's literacy and critical awareness eventually developed, as shown in his distinguished service as a member of Parliament (sixty-four years), being prime minister, and rich, voluminous writings (Nobel Prize for literature, 1953). All of that has less to do with home studies than his Harrow schooling, self-education, and burning ambition to make his name after graduating from Sandhurst. Doubtlessly, his nanny deserves tremendous credit for his socio-emotional integrity and balance; no small feat given the parents. As I see it, playing her role as a stand-in rather than as a rival to the parents, she could form binding attachment with the boys that they transferred to their parents. Since Mrs. Everest cared for the boys as a nanny instead of being a blood kin, there seems to be an object lesson for teachers here, which is to maintain objectivity as well as warmth in guiding children. Several years ago, there was news of a teacher who became so enamored with a thirteen-year-old student that she ran off with him to Mexico.

Biographer Roy Jenkins wrote that, "Winston Churchill's non-relationship with his father was even more wistful than was his semi-relationship with his mother…It is one of supreme ironies that now, more than a century after his death, he (Randolph) should be best known as a father" (page 10). However, I have the strong suspicion that Winston's heroics as a young soldier and historic achievements came about in large part through his desire to disprove his father's great disappointment in him.

Lance Armstrong (1971-)

Lance Armstrong won the Tour de France cycling race for the seventh time in 2005, a feat that had never been done before. Returning to racing in January 2009, he finished third in the Tour de France. With twelve stages remaining in the 2010 Tour, which he said would be his last, a crash ended Lance's hopes for another victory. Dedicated to excruciating, disciplined training and racing, he was raised by a most devoted, single-minded mother. Saying "we grew up together," Linda was only seventeen when Lance was born. After the father left them two years later, Linda worked as a supermarket check-out clerk, a realtor, and a telecommunications company account manager.

After he was ranked as the world's best cyclist and named a member of the U.S. Olympic cycling team in 1996, Lance learned that he suffered advanced cancer, which he fought to a successful recovery. Linda remarried and divorced once again. Lance and Kristin Richard, the mother of his three children, married in 1997 during his trying struggle with cancer. It was the same year that he founded the Lance Armstrong Foundation, which funds cancer research and provides support for cancer victims, a charitable enterprise displaying Lance's good side.

Because of Kristin's distaste for his all-consuming training and celebrity and having to be constantly on the move from one nation and abode to another, they divorced in 2003. That same year, Lance began to date Sheryl Crow, a nine-time Grammy winning blues rock singer. After declaring their engagement in 2005, they broke up in February 2006. Many friendships have been destroyed by Lance's driving ambition to win, reckless quirks, and unforgiving temper. No matter what, Linda has never second-guessed her son's actions. Mother and son formed an attachment that was a stronghold unto themselves, in which Linda's managing style of Lance was no doubt indulgent-permissive.

Although there is a storybook tale of Linda's struggle to survive and support her son and Lance's historic
supremacy in the tough, competitive cycling grind, many
who have confronted his personality traits have become
thoroughly disillusioned with him. Describing an ugly
confrontation with cyclist Filippo Simeoni that Lance
maliciously provoked on the last run of a race that he
had already won, Daniel Coyle (pages 286–287) wrote
that Lance received widespread condemnation for his
poor sportsmanship. *Procycling* magazine said his act
was "a moment revealing all of the champion's cunning
and ruthlessness, that will forever color memories of his
career." *Bicycling* magazine stated, "The ugliest side … of
the race's grandest champion." Doping charges rose again
against Armstrong in August 2010 when a former team
member accused Lance and other team members of using
blood transfusions and performance-enhancing drugs.

Mae West (1893–1980)

Many believe that there has been no entertainer more
flamboyant and hyperactive than Mae West. With her
trademark line, "Why don't you come up and see me
sometime?" intoned in her unique, saucy voice, Mae West
is remembered "as the pop archetype of sexual wantonness
and ribald humor" (from Jill Watts' book jacket). I have
enjoyed her movies for their racy, raucous satire, especially
when costarring with bulbous-nosed W.C. Fields. In
boisterous set-tos, Mae always had comebacks that spun
him into conniptions, scenes that she may have scripted
herself.

Mae West spent decades on the stage. She danced and sang in vaudeville and challenged anti-smut laws of the times with daring productions that she put together. City ordinances forced many to close. Mae also wrote many pulp bestsellers, such as *The Constant Sinner* (1931). She had success with long-running shows on or near Broadway and on cross-country tours with lead roles for herself, as in "Diamond Lil." Her favorite routine was the shimmy, a jazz dance with vigorous shaking of the body from the shoulders down, which she adopted from her great interest in African-American culture and music. Far ahead of her time, West advocated equality for blacks and had Hollywood studios include them in her movies, such as Louis Armstrong, who was popular in Harlem clubs in the 1920s, but unknown by whites.

By 1949, national polls showed that her popularity equaled that of Eleanor Roosevelt. In *Sex, Health, and ESP* (1975), a book that she published at age eighty-two, she gave her recipe for long life. West said that she "rechanneled her sex drive into pure energy that propelled her through all tasks. She encouraged readers to strip off their clothes, lie in bed, think about sex, and, once the 'urges' increased, set off to work" (page 306). Making it pay off in fortune and fame, Mae latched on to a sex-teasing theme when still a child performer.

Born in Brooklyn to John and Tillie West, The father worked as a policeman, a prizefighter with the name "'Battlin' Jack West," watchman, and private detective. John had a volatile temper and was usually absent from his family, as he dashed in and out of the house and spent nights carousing. His ties with the underworld got him work and openings for Mae. As no one in the family

dared to say anything whenever he was present, little Mae
no doubt sat mimicking her father's thunder to herself.

After Mae toured with a stock company and gradually
went out on her own, her close bond with her mom, the
family's stalwart, continued by phone, letters, reunions,
and their shrewd investments and underworld alliances.
Tillie came to manage the Harding Hotel near Times
Square with an annual rent gross of $700,000, which
came about from the family's ties with Owney Madden, New York's crime boss and generous Robin Hood to
many. Madden funded many legitimate enterprises, such
as the hotel, and helped to promote Mae's career.

In 1928, Tillie developed cancer that doctors could not
stop from spreading.

> To cheer her, Mae brought several of "The Pleasure
> Man's" female impersonators out to Long Island
> for visits. One did her hair, and another made her
> extravagant hats, one of her greatest passions.
> Additionally, Mae showered her mother with
> gifts—gowns, purses, and more hats. (Sister) Beverly
> observed, "It kept both of their spirits up" (page 114).
> "As 'Diamond Lil's' engagement in Los Angeles
> came to a close, Mae received word that the cancer
> had spread to Tillie's liver and that she was dying.
> She hired a private train and on January 14, 1929,
> immediately after her last performance, departed
> with the company, racing to Brooklyn, where Tillie
> was being cared for... With her devoted daughter
> nearby, Tillie West, the force that had nurtured an
> American folk icon, passed away (page 117).

In contrast, when Mae's father died six years later, "West's
reaction to his passing was markedly detached" (page

199). She only took an afternoon off for his funeral and was filming again the next day.

James Bryant Conant (1893–1978)

Scientist, Harvard University President, and prominent public servant, James Conant accomplished much during his life. Following World War I service as an Army poison gas chemist, he joined Harvard in 1919 as a chemistry professor. Before Harvard selected Conant for its president in 1933, his research and teaching in organic and physical chemistry had received a long list of awards, capped by the Priestley Medal in 1944, the highest honor of the American Chemical Society.

Harvard's President for twenty years to 1953, Conant turned a clubby school for upper-class New Englanders into a premier research university, which it remains today. Stressing student merit and intellectual promise more than social and alumni connections, he introduced aptitude tests into undergraduate admissions, and other colleges followed suit. Conant thus spurred development of the SAT that is widely used in college admissions today. He converted Harvard's undergraduate curriculum from the classics to modern subjects, and urged professors to conduct research and involve students as learner-partners as he had done. Harvard's world-class standing today can be largely traced to his leadership.

From 1941–1946, James Conant chaired the National Defense Research Committee, which meant that he administered the Manhattan Project that built the atomic bomb. He alone held "responsibility for considering the new weapon's long-range scientific, political, diplomatic, and military implications, and acted as intermediary between the White House on the one hand, and on the other the scientists, industrialists, and military men involved in the vast covert undertaking" (Hershberg, page 5). Those responsibilities called for a scientist-administrator of rare organizational ability and he fulfilled the herculean job effectively. Following the war, he remained in the inner group advising the Truman White House on nuclear, Cold War issues, and also the National Science Foundation and Atomic Energy Commission. Although Conant helped to build the atomic bomb to end World War II, he later fought the building of the hydrogen bomb because he feared its massive destructiveness could endanger human existence. During the red-baiting hysteria of the 1950s, although he did not criticize Senator Joseph McCarthy by name, Conant denounced the "irrational mob spirit" of fear-mongering conservatives, whose activities he said endangered American freedoms. Writing tirelessly on education, such as *Education and Liberty: The Role of the Schools in a Modern Democracy* (1952), he championed equality of opportunity for women, uplifting the quality of schools, and support to public education. In 1953, he resigned the Harvard presidency to become U.S. High Commissioner and Ambassador to Germany, a complex post he held until 1957 when he retired.

How could he perform so many tasks so well at the same time, even to find time to teach students at Harvard and other colleges through arduous duties in Cambridge, Washington, and wherever? Conant's wife, Patty, answered that question by calling him a "jet-propelled missile." Conant's childhood and youth help to answer the question. His middle-class parents, James Scott and

Jennett Orr, traced their ancestry to the Mayflower and Salem. But they differed from other New Englanders in that their "political and religious views … strayed from the de rigueur Boston combination of Republicanism and Protestantism (Unitarian, Episcopalian, and Congregational) … (and young James) was thereby encouraged to take a relatively open-minded approach to issues." The young boy's "parents were Swedenborgians, members of a religious sect that blended scientific inquiry and mysticism … (believing) that systematic measurement and investigation of nature could lead one to the miraculous and the divine." The sect pursued "math, physics, anatomy, astronomy, and chemistry to theological illumination and a firm belief in immortality" (Hershberg, page 13). Before the lad became six, however, his parents' faith in the sect's mysticism faded, but the family continued to embody puritan ethics of orderliness, work, reason, and pragmatism to the fullest.

He applied those traits as Harvard's president, and more so in Washington, D.C. Though he abided by Harvard's faculty-administration cordiality and consensus in the main, exigencies in how the government handled World War II and the Cold War with multiple, overlapping agencies and interests called for decisive, informed leadership. Two close chemist friends, who knew him through the many complicated nuclear issues, called him an "unemotional, cold Yankee" and one who used a "cold logical approach" to decisions (Hershberg, page 475).

The father had a photoengraving business and amazed the boy with its technology. The father also impressed his son by developing technical innovations that advanced the business, as well as to satisfy their mutual curiosity.

By ten, through close association with his father, James had developed a strong interest in experimenting, which the father stimulated further by building young Conant a makeshift lab, equipped with basic instruments and providing the youngster a monthly allowance of $5 to buy supplies. James supplemented his allowance by charging neighborhood five cents each to watch his chemical tricks and their bright flashes.

Conant's attachment and social interaction with his father and his experimental efforts came to mind on news of the 2006 Nobel Prize in chemistry, awarded to Roger Kornberg of Stanford University's School of Medicine for his breakthrough explanation of how cells in living organisms use the genetic information on DNA. Forty-seven years earlier in 1959, Roger's father, Arthur, also a Stanford professor, had won the Nobel Prize in physiology-medicine. The Kornberg's are the eighth parent and child to become Nobel laureates. Arthur often took his three children with him to his laboratory where they watched their dad conduct research, and tinkered about on their own. Seated together during their interview on PBS' News-Hour, October 4, 2006, the father reported that when he asked ten-year-old Roger what he wanted for a Christmas present, Roger answered, "A week in the lab."

While dignified stoicism characterized the father, James' opinionated mother, Jennett, ruled the household with the supporting chorus of the boy's grandmother, aunts, female cousin, and two sisters, "the regiment of women who watched over my growing up" (page 14). Jennett and her sisters vigorously opposed slavery and followed "Grandfather (William Jennings) Bryant" in being Democrats and opponents to what they saw as "the

imperialism of the Republicans' Spanish American War."
Enthused with the war as other boys, however, young
James cheered the fray. As time passed, his sociopoliti-
cal views approximated his mother's. No doubt, Jennett's
strong social views and willingness to express them reinforced the boy's "lively inquisitiveness" that father James
Scott also stimulated. Reflecting tolerance for differences
of opinion, "the regiment of women," as he described
them, allowed him to prance about with play uniform and
popgun and applaud Teddy Roosevelt's Cuban exploits.
The chief feature of Conant's attachment with his parents
and kin is how they engaged his thinking and encouraged faith and independence of mind. Their rich, fluid
give-and-take interaction shows that the family management style was authoritative-engaging, the best approach
as chapter two discussed.

Comparisons and Contrasts

Now that we have put a magnifying glass on the ten
individuals' childhoods and lives, each one memorable
and real, let's assess them further by comparing and contrasting them on key concepts. As said at the start of this
chapter, the aim is to illustrate and enlarge upon what was
discussed in preceding chapters. The ten persons selected
provide a varied, thought-provoking group for much
opportunity to relate childhood with adulthood. For
besides their having quite diverse parents, household conditions, and schooling, they matured as adults with mostly
unpredictable results.   A psychologist and reader of
biographies, I appreciate authors, such as Ted Kennedy,
who present lots of information about their subjects'

families, and childhood relations with their parents and teachers. Autobiographies by the person himself or herself, such as Maria Trapp's, can raise questions, because sugar coating cannot be dismissed. For every person, childhood is not only a time of tremendous physiological growth and change, but also when each individual's mind and personality begin to develop. Unfortunately, because many caregivers are ignorant of what should be done and avoid, the emotional and mental development of children is often shortchanged and tragically, even harmed permanently. What I am advocating is not so much producing geniuses and billionaires as it is to develop people with fulfilling lives who can think effectively and find happiness within themselves and with others, and can pass the same to their own children.

Suppose there was a rise in human qualities and civilization each year; imagine what a better world there would be. It grieves me that after eons of discourse on what is holy, good, true, and beautiful, humankind has not progressed much in the fulfillment of universal ideals and values. With prisons overflowing and bloodshed and tensions today as in the past and present, it can be argued that human evolution may be reverting. Never mind technological progress—what we need are real advances in mind and heart. Social advances seem hardest to achieve, as the news is awash with war, sex, pornography, drugs, crime, political dissension, and corporate corruption. What can be expected by 2050, when children born today have lived most of their lives, and in 2100 for their offspring? Forging a chasm between reality and ideal that widens threateningly, the shortcomings of society and institutions compare miserably with our ideals. The best and noble we ever seem to see are typically humanitarian and security actions and services that follow warfare, disasters, and crime; being ex post facto means that crises and lawlessness take precedence. *Raising and Teaching Young Children for Their Tomorrows* was written with the conviction that childhood is when a real difference in humanity can be made. That is the responsibility of parents, relatives and teachers. Alison Gopnik put it well:

> Our children give point and purpose to our lives…They are at the root of our deepest moral dilemmas and greatest moral triumphs. We care more about our children than we do about ourselves. Our children live on after we are gone, and this gives us a kind of immortality.

As our review of ten lives shows, there are great differences in how children are raised and what sorts of people they become as adults. That comes from caregivers' education, wealth or poverty, childhood experiences of their own, etc. Also influential is the fact that many parents raise their children with homespun opinions that can be wrongheaded and contradictory. Instead of seat-of-the-pants childcare, like letting people act on Broadway and perform surgery without adequate training and experience, far better results would come from sound knowledge and skill.

Born free in mind and spirit, children absorb ideas, attitudes, love, hate, language, etc., from their close ones, much of which sticks indelibly through their lives. Therefore, through the crucible of childhood and youth, parents, teachers, and their social and physical environments shape humanity, which begins anew with the birth of each baby. Through many years of care and guidance then, parents, relatives, and teachers have the wondrous opportunity to surpass all that they can do in their lives by raising and teaching children properly to high qualities of mind and heart. Cheapening childhood not only robs youths of their fullest potentials, but stays the status quo in human evolution. While scientific-technological advances proliferate to provide greater health and convenience, humaneness and wisdom do not advance. Cell phones, PCs, etc., are very helpful, but do they affect advances in human character and morals?

As Leo Tolstoy wrote in his novel, *Anna Karenina* (1877), "Hypocrisy in anything whatever may deceive the cleverest and most penetrating man, but the least wide-awake of children recognizes it, and is revolted by it, however ingeniously it may be disguised." Since students and my own children have taught me much, I sense what Tolstoy meant. But he may have gone overboard with that generalization. Although youngsters can be quick in questioning the actions and decisions of others, what they would do and decide instead is often impractical and critical for the sake of criticizing. Quixotically, however, Tolstoy's novel begins with the following line: "Happy families are all alike; every unhappy family is unhappy in its own way." As his novel is about Anna Karenina and her family and pursuers, with the central theme being how difficult it is to be honest to oneself when everyone else accepts falseness, I interpret Tolstoy's statement broadly to mean that well-functioning families and individuals are equipped to avoid and solve problems should they arise; everything seems to be working for them. Since the path to progress and happiness can be fraught with dangers, vigilance coupled with faith and sound problem-solving tactics help to keep the ship afloat and sailing straight and true, which the authoritative-engaging style can manage best.

Attachment and Social Interaction

Our survey uncovered a variety of caregiver-child attachments. Lance Armstrong's and Mae West's attachments with their mothers were the most tightly bound, as offspring and mothers went in lockstep. The two bonds are quite different. Lance Armstrong's mother, Linda, maintained a highly protective and exclusive attachment, like a fortress. As Daniel Coyle wrote: "Mother and son lived together inside a capsule of forward momentum, never looking back" (pages 288–289). In contrast, Mae's attachment with Tillie, her mother, was inclusive and receptive to others, like an open door. Lance's twice-divorced mother raised him by herself and labored hard to provide for their needs, while Mae's family remained relatively fixed and secure. Also, Lance's obsession about winning and his exacting, lonely training and hot-tempered reaction to defeat and dissention stand worlds apart from Mae's hilarity, grandstanding, and abundant relationships with others. Chiefly because of the sharp contrasts in the mothers and their situations, the tightly-bound attachments of the West's and Armstrong's generated contrasting social interaction—never-ending gabbing between Mae and Tillie versus Lance's and Linda's comparative reserve.

Tillie treated Mae as if she was fulfilling her own aspirations of being a stage star. After Mae won some amateur contests, the mother arranged vaudeville spots for her little five-year-old, and they were on their way. Tillie labored painstakingly on Mae's costumes and got Jack to haul Mae's suitcase to theaters. Learning early on that risqué acts by the little girl had a shock effect that raised applause and notice, Tillie exploited the sex theme, which had a lifelong effect on Mae. They studied and copied the performances of popular vaudevillians, such as Eva Tanguay, who "knew how to manipulate male spectators and enact desirability" (Watts, page 17). In contrast, Linda had no active role to play in Lance's lonely training and races.

Maternal bonding with babies is universal, a natural, motherly trait which humans share with other mammals. Dennis Dixon, University of Oregon's outstanding quarterback, misses his mother, who died of breast cancer in 2004, and their strong attachment so much that he had her image tattooed on his arm and carries a medallion with her photo. Although all of us might not go for tattooing, we can sympathize with his sincere feelings for his mom. It says much that many soldiers in their death throes, whatever their nationality, cry out for their mothers: mom, mére, ma, Mutter, okasan, mat,' madre, madar, mataji, etc. That "mother" is voiced much alike across the world underlines the universal nature side of being human, as is somewhat true for "father": dad, papa, túva, Vatter, otosan, baba, babbo, etc. One explanation for the universal similarity of mothers' names is that they relate to babies' sucking instincts. If so, what's the origin of fathers' names?

Without a doubt, Mae West's and her mother's attachment and social interaction would rank among the most positive and constructively enduring in a representative sample. With mutual mindedness, I see their interaction beating so rhythmically together that they could finish each other's sentences. Their MAC bond, which brought both of them fortune and enriched lives, contrasts like night and day with Mae's superficial relationship with her father.

While mother-child attachment and social interaction are typically positive and strongest of caregivers, they can be negative, as in the cases of John F. Kennedy and Winston Churchill, both through neglect. JFK's situation seems to have affected him much more than Winston's because of Rose's stern, cold demeanor, and the fact that Churchill had Mrs. Everest for a dear nanny, who convinced the boy to believe that his parents loved him. JFK's older brother, Joseph Jr., the other Kennedy children, and household servants, of whom biographers regretfully tell us nothing about, undoubtedly gave JFK nurturance and balance. Social interaction with a loving, paternalistic father and a cold, reserved mother can produce contradictory, split-hearted attachment for children. Biographers don't go into it much, but I believe that the Kennedy brood compensated for their insecure parental attachment through their famously close sibling ties. Jack worshipped his older brother, Joseph Jr., and tried to emulate him in every way, and he also enjoyed and relied on the uncompromising loyalty and support of his brothers and sisters.

Maternal bonds can be impotent and lack depth, as it was for Robert Hanssen, whose mother loved him, but always gave in to the boy's brutish father and did not shelter Bob. If any paternal attachment developed during Bob's infancy, it couldn't have survived beyond age three or four, as indicated by the harsh, father-dominated social interaction described in the bio sketch above. Social interaction with his mother constricted into soothing but empty routines and gestures. What materialized was

negative detachment and social interaction with everyone other than with his kids and Bonnie, whom he married in 1968. Throughout Bob's upbringing when his
father's domineering manner held absolute center stage,
his mother's wimpy presence was complicit. Similar to
Robert and Vivian Hanssen, Adolf Hitler's attachment
and social interaction with his mother, Klara, were also
affectionate, but empty of meaning and direction. By
overindulging Adolf's peculiarities, even allowing the boy
to drop out of school and remain idle, it was as if Klara
never stopped treating him as an infant. In both cases, the
shallow social interaction between mother and child never
rose above the mundane and angst toward father. However, the extreme contrasting influence of Hanssen's and
Hitler's authoritarian fathers and their indulgent mothers
raises the question as to whether the divide manifested
the worst of both.

The future Führer's attachment and social interaction
with his mother inculcated him with narcissism and conceit that led to megalomania. In contrast to the superior
mothers in our review, both Hitler's and Hanssen's mothers were pitifully fainthearted. Of course, the two women
feared their husbands, but it's impossible to imagine Tillie West and other strong moms surrendering their kids
and themselves to harsh tyranny. Hitler's father died when
Adolf was fourteen, and Bob's father, who lived to retirement, remained a thorn in his son's hide for long. Adolf's
mother died when he was still a teenager at eighteen, and
Bob's lived to old age. While it probably would not have
made a difference for Adolf if his parents had lived on,
Bob might have turned out better if he had lost his parents at an earlier age and was sent to decent kinfolks, if

any. As the highly honored Nazi-hunter Simon Wiesen-
thal said: "No one is born criminal."

Developmental psychologists have concluded that
indifferent-neglectful and permissive-indulgent caregivers are the poorest in raising children. Authoritarian-
raised youth have the advantage of being given some
direction and identity, though often errant. Almost anything their youths do and say go unheeded by neglectful
parents, and are tolerated by indulgent parents. Admon-
ishments by indulgent mothers, such as "Please don't do
that," and "Oh my, what have we here?" are ignored by
their children. One indulgent mother, who brought her
mischievous children to play with ours, scolded them by
saying, "I won't love you if you keep that up," and "I'm
going to pack my bags and leave you if you don't behave!"
As they paid no attention to her at all, they trashed our
playpen and my son's prized scooter.

We found positive paternal attachment and social
interaction in the childhoods of Sandra Day O'Connor,
Henry James Jr., JFK, the Trapp children, and James
Conant. Praised for her pragmatic, compromising
approach to the law, O'Connor's judicial career reflects
her down-to-earth youth during which she was especially attached to her outdoors-working father at the
Lazy-B-Ranch. Henry James's writings and life reflect
the intellectual, probing influence of his intense, varied-
minded father and a household that teemed with ideas
and debate—how unlike the family social interaction of
Hanssen's and Hitler's households. Repeating what has
been said earlier about the dominating paternalism of
Jack Kennedy's father, the bond between JFK and Joseph
Sr. can be assessed as mainly positive because Jack and

his brothers and sisters realized that their father cared for them, as he did all he could to assist and direct them. I read once that Joseph said that he would use his wealth to promote JFK's election as president, but he also said, "I'm not going to pay for a landslide." Until Maria entered their lives, the Trapp children also faced dominating paternalism. Their widower father often traveled, leaving his brood to servants and dictating his regulations on dress and conduct before he departed. Saying that von Trapp's paternalism followed Austrian tradition, Maria said he softened through her faith and positive attachment and social interaction with the children.

James Conant believed that people are born with or without intelligence, in other words, that children's nurture and environment had little to do with their abilities. He had little faith in the belief of educators that many poor learners could be late bloomers and succeed as they mature. Conant's parents warmly welcomed and encouraged his curiosity and talents. His mind and future success grew out of his parents' guidance, and the buoyancy of the family's broad interests and their faith shift from Swedenborgianism to Puritanism. In short, if Conant analyzed how he was reared and taught, he might have said that everything fitted together—innate intelligence and curiosity to start with, parents and kin who nurtured him with love and encouragement, and excellent teachers, one particularly, all of whom provided him independence of mind and a steady outpouring of ideas and dedication to reason and science. Thus, Conant was the product of excellent MAC attachment, faith, and highly stimulating social interaction.

Lance Armstrong never got to know his birth father and turned his back on his adoptive father, Terry Armstrong, whom his mother divorced, which reflects on Lance's and Linda's exclusive bond. As Lance put it, divorce "... tears kids up and yet we're kicking this guy out and [I'm] ecstatic" (Coyle, page 290). Seldom paying attention to his son, Randolph Churchill constantly criticized Winston, yet the son always stayed true and respectful to his father, as well as to his also absentee mother; love for his parents, which has been said arose from his nanny's guidance as a dedicated go-between instead of parental rival.

Our bio study shows that attachment and social interaction are often more positive between children and one parent—O'Connor, Hanssen, Hitler, Armstrong, and West. With the exceptions of JFK's case and what Maria Trapp wrote about von Trapp's relationship with his children before and after she joined the family, father-children bonds are not as strong as those of mothers and children. That is hardly surprising, given mothers' traditional roles and nature's influence. As Robert Frost wrote, "You don't have to deserve your mother's love. You have to deserve your father's. He's more particular." Also, Quentin Crisp wrote, "My mother protected me from the world and my father threatened me with it."

Notable is the finding that equivalent positive attachments and social interaction between both parents and children came up least often in our sample—Henry James Jr. and James B. Conant. Both sets of parents are outstanding in being admirably bound themselves with mutual compatibility and affection, which no doubt facilitated their close relations with their children. America's thirty-second President, Franklin D. Roosevelt, also enjoyed a cherubic childhood, with parents he both adored and who loved him. Functioning in ensemble rather than in conflict with each other, parents of James, Conant, and FDR played complementary roles. While James' father led and stimulated the family with his ideas and intellectual activities, his mother was, as James wrote, "'so widely open yet so softly-enclosing lap' of his father's 'liberties and all our securities'... 'She *was* he, *was* each of us'" (Edel, pages 13–14). It resembled Conant's positive relations with both of his parents. What follows from Conrad Black's excellent biography of FDR (pages 15–16) also underlines what we are discussing here as well as childhood's lasting effects:

> (While FDR's) father taught and accompanied him in sports, his mother was a benign but unswerving figure of authority in almost all other things. Franklin knew only the tyranny of his mother's regimental routine. There was no spontaneity, variety, privacy, or unpredictability... For such an intelligent child, faced with such a loving but strict mother, the choice between rebellion, submission, and the application of guile was constantly to be made... He gradually developed the skill of placatory acceptance of his mother's authority, tempered by as much leeway as he could carve out for himself. Many of the mundane political acts he would perfect, including obfuscation, prevarication, flattery, sophistical evasion, and various forms of pandering, were developed and tested on an involuntary focus group of one, whose acuity was far above the mean.

Perhaps not surprising because of the firm nature of most men as compared to the natural tenderness of most women, the worst parent-child ties were with fathers—

Hanssen, Hitler, Churchill, Armstrong, and West. However, O'Connor's close attachment and social interaction with her father prevent any hard and fast generalization. Today's father-children role relations are more positively structured than in the past—a healthy development. Some fathers today willingly accept being house dads, while mothers take or share the role of breadwinner, and to my delight, many take ample time to engage their kids in activities.

Learning Readiness and Awareness

Because biographies often bypass or are sketchy about subjects' education and conscious awareness during their early years, we have less information on those factors to consider than on attachment and social interaction, except for James Conant, whose child rearing equated learning readiness and awareness. Both parents encouraged James' precocity by their habit of reasoning and abiding by puritan values, which as I speculate did not go much for lots of empty kisses and "I love you(s)," but did reward thought and deeds. Although James Hershberg related little that connects directly to attachment and social interaction (he wrote that Conant's autobiography, *My Several Lives: Memoirs of a Social Inventor* (1970) is silent on his personal life and family), everything he wrote about the parents' and household's attention to Conant's thinking, learning readiness, and awareness indicates that the boy enjoyed most positive, authoritative-engaging attachment and social interaction with his parents and relatives. After Jennett intervened for his son's enrollment in the prestigious Roxbury Latin School, pleading successfully that his sci-

entific talents and interests far outweighed then weaknesses in math and writing, James met "the teacher who
had the greatest influence on my life"—Newton Henry
Black. Black soon saw that James had abundant curiosity
and scientific talent, and gave freely of his time to guide
the young man toward his future scientific career. "At
Black's side Conant absorbed physics and chemistry lore,
fingered advanced texts, honed experimental techniques,
and adopted his mentor's instinctual quest for empirical
data rather than argument to attach difficult questions"
(page 16). Broad, far-reaching transfer of learning like that
has magical characteristics. As we shall also see shortly
with Winston Churchill and Robert Somervell and
Henry James and John La Farge, the great worth of excellent teachers who have the knack of enlightening youth
with keen insight and know-how, and attending to their
skills and cognitive development cannot be overstated.

Sandra O'Connor was highly interested and involved
in activities of her father's Lazy-B-Cattle Ranch in southeastern Arizona, and read constantly with study help
from her mother. Benefiting from thirteen years of good
schooling in El Paso, and inspiration from her loving,
church-going grandmother, young O'Connor had good
learning readiness and awareness before going to Stanford University, where she has said her mind opened up
to the world. Stanford Law School prepared her for an
historic legal career. Her eagerness to work alongside her
father and the cowboys indicate wide-eyed readiness to
learn and develop awareness. That she achieved so well at
the elite university shows that her awareness and learning
enlarged through higher education and meeting diverse

others of intellect. Sandra enthusiastically credits Stanford's professors for developing her mind and knowledge.

As a boy, John Kennedy already had a sharp mind. Although not outstanding at school, JFK focused on and followed his special interests and tried to keep up with his older brother, Joe Jr. Dallek (page 30) reports that a missionary's talk on India one morning stirred the schoolboy to learn more about the world and created the desire to help improve it. Sent to Canterbury School in New Milford, Connecticut, an exclusive Catholic academy with fourteen teachers for only ninety-two students, Jack wrote his parents how homesick and cold he felt and that he did well in English, math, and history, but poorly in science and Latin, having a "C" average grade. When well enough from his ailments, Jack pursued spirited sports with his siblings. The family's far-reaching journeys and competitive tone can be interpreted as windows to uplifting awareness and perspective.

Jack's learning readiness and awareness as a youth more or less conformed to his father's demands for competitive effort and his mother's dictates to do well and maintain decorum. Obviously, their father's diverse businesses and political activities, and their mother's strong faith and connections with popes and cardinals, provided extraordinary amplification for their brood's exposure to and awareness of ideas, people, and the world. It also bred arrogant snobbery. JFK's perceptions and knowledge were undoubtedly enlarged by provocative experiences that very few young people can possibly have, especially during Joe's ambassadorship to Britain and Jack's naval service when he encountered diverse persons and groups, particularly ordinary Joes.

Both Robert Hanssen and Adolf Hitler were defiant students. They had intelligence, but their warped attitudes toward school and everything created mental blocks. Showing brilliance at times, Hanssen usually did only enough to pass, but his academic record was good enough for him to be accepted by Northwestern University's dental school and MBA program. Stubbornly refusing to conform, Hitler dropped out of school. Although he had little education, even in art in which he claimed to have talent, Hitler grasped control of the Nazi Party through chicanery and raving speechmaking. Raised by sadistic fathers and weak, indulgent mothers, the two grew up terribly awry and came to personify degradation. Between the fathers' authoritarianism and the mothers' indulgence, the two manifested the worst of both managing styles.

Split parental alliances can interfere with children's learning readiness and awareness. Even when families have satisfactory fathers, there are mothers who form alliances of a petty nature against the fathers with their offspring, like Hitler's and Hanssen's mothers. While less likely, similar father-children alliances that stand off mothers are also possible. Because Mae West's dad was a clod and mostly absent, Mae's bond with her mom was not directed in hostility toward Jack West, as she and Tillie used him to advance their enterprises. A saying I once tested scientifically and found valid is, "Two is company; three is a crowd." Because of normal parents' love for each other and are united in their roles with their children, that old saying does not relate to most families. Still, having only one child, a pet favorite out of a brood, or being a single parent can lead to us-versus-them conceit and narrow-mindedness.

It could be that Lance Armstrong's limited education and stormy conflicts with advisors, supporters, and competitors; legal battles; divorce with Kristin Richard, mother of his three children; and his breakup with star singer Sheryl Crow, all stem from a too-confined attachment with his mother. Although Linda had backbone that Klara and Vivian lacked, when training and racing interfered with his education, Linda allowed Lance to drop out of Plano East Senior High at age seventeen. But later on, he graduated from the Bending Oaks Private Academy in Dallas; his formal education ending there. Focused almost totally on Lance's racing history, Coyle tells nothing about how Linda raised her son. However, everything about Lance, especially his volatile personality, indicates that Linda's managing style was permissive-indulgent.

Winston Churchill has had the reputation of being a poor student, but Roy Jenkins says that although the boy was deficient in math, Greek, and Latin, "he had exceptional interest in and aptitude for the use of the English language," which better teachers recognized. Recalling his demotion to a class for underachievers in his memoirs, *My Early Life* (1930), Churchill praised Robert Somervell, an English teacher, for teaching him how to write English—complimenting him as "a most delightful man, to whom my debt is great" (Jenkins, page 18). Winston's memory was phenomenal, such as reciting twelve hundred lines of Macaulay's *Lays of Ancient Rome* faultlessly, which won him a prize at Harrow School. As said earlier, the boy's early years under his nanny's care and his resistance to his gov-

erness probably delayed his learning readiness and ill-prepared him for the strict, classical schooling of those days.

The learning readiness and awareness of Henry James
Jr. came by way of his unique sensitive, observational
power, which his novels reflect so well. The family's buzz-
ing colloquy, thought-provoking friends and visitors, and
numerous travels to Europe, stirred the young man's readiness to learn and stay alert. Trying to shelter his brood
from dogmatic, rigid schooling, the father enrolled Junior
and his siblings at many different schools. The father's
religious views were also eclectic, so that young Henry
would write when an adult that his upbringing gave him
"no standard by which to judge the facts of the life he
saw around him. Reflecting on his youth, he said that felt
forced to attend to everything and by that process could
find "order, reason and common sense into the world's
chaos." Ebel continued,

> James was struck by his isolation (in school). The little
> boy was as shy in class as, at home. He neither attracted
> attention, nor was molested by his thoroughly down-
> to-earth schoolfellows. He gives the impression that
> he was perturbed by this, yet at the same time, aware
> of the ground upon which he stood as a little observer
> of the human scene (page 37).

Artist John La Farge recognized James' sensitivity to
details and people, and a gift of putting his observations
into words. They met in the artist's studio, where James
realized he could not draw well. Befriending the young
man, La Farge encouraged him to read the works of
Honoré de Balzac, who had founded the realist school of
writing with intuitive observations of thousands of char-

acters and places. The artist urged James to write and use words as if painting. As "La Farge had appeared in his life at a significant moment" (Ebel, page 55), serving as his life's most important teacher, few novelists have benefited more from their early experiences and contacts.

References for Maria Trapp, Lance Armstrong, and Mae West tell nothing about their early learning readiness and awareness, but we can make some inferences. Concentrating on getting ahead in her world of stage and movies, Mae was always alert and receptive to ideas and opportunity. On stage as a seven-year-old, she relished the thrill of audience applause for her racy acts. She and Tillie expanded Mae's youthful success with the risqué into a lifelong theme. Energetically writing novels and scripts between acts and shows, Mae labored to expand her mind and literacy. On tour with stock companies as a youth with two shows daily, six days a week, her formal schooling never went far. Work and colleagues became her teachers, and she made the most of diverse roles, from Shakespeare to melodramas. Watts wrote,

> All the plays influenced her, but she was most intrigued by melodrama. With plots pitting good against evil, this genre required distinctive acting techniques. Performers ranted their lines, underscoring their delivery with exaggerated body language. Dialogue was Spartan, and players wrung the most from each word. Mae remembered how 'we played it earnestly and swiftly, and we did what we could to learn our parts better and make our acting say more than the lines could.' Although she was a hellion, Mae was a perceptive child and a prodigious mimic (page 20).

Tillie would have approved of that, saying, "You betcha, that's my girl"!

As we approach the end of this chapter, the management styles of the ten characters' families deserve summary. Hanssen and Hitler had authoritarian-dictatorial fathers and indulgent-permissive mothers. Authoritative-engaging parents, grandmother, and ranch hands raised O'Connor. Not easy to characterize, JFK had a mostly authoritarian father and a distant, neglectful mother, but his many siblings provided loving attachment and social interaction. West's father was dictatorial, but usually absent, while Mae and mom had a MAC attachment that flourished with their authoritative-engaging social interaction. Armstrong's mother managed the boy with permissiveness and a life them-versus-us attitude. Conant and James luxuriated from their large households' affectionate authoritative-engaging style of managing them. With indifferent-neglectful parents, Churchill fortunately was raised by his nanny's authoritative-engaging style.

Child development involves psychological and physical growth, with the former being the most important. Parents who regard their young children as precious, but mentally inert and void, are badly mistaken; those who neglect and abuse their youths are shamefully undeserving and harming their children's emotional development. Our survey of ten individuals' young and adult lives found great differences in raising and teaching children and how their best or worst potentials came to being. I hope that readers will pursue biographies with special attention to the subjects' childhoods. To hammer that point down, here are two more.

George Washington (1732–1799)

I have read numerous works about Washington, most dealing with his being Commander-in-Chief of the Revolutionary Army. Biographers tell little of his childhood, because records are slim. His respected father, who divided his estate fairly among his boys, died when George was ten. Little is said about his mother, except that she was strict and favored him out of her six children. Fifteen years older and educated in England, his half-brother and a colonial officer, Lawrence, recognized the boy's intelligence and "perfect rectitude," and took George under his wings. Young George attached himself to his brother as a manly model of good mind and manners, and his being a military hero. Without a doubt, bonding with Lawrence and his engaging style set the path of America's first president toward his historic leadership roles. Positive attachments of importance for children then are not necessarily limited to the earliest years or to parents. As role models shape the thought and behavior of those who look up to them, much transfer of learning can be generated of the type that often asks what would he or she do and think in this or that situation. What people gain from role models can go further than just mere imitation.

Matthew Arnold (1822–1866)

Arnold was born into a religious, well-educated, and outgoing family in England with many relatives and friends, such as poet William Wordsworth, who stimulated intellectual discourse and interests. His father served as headmaster of Rugby School, one of the England's prominent schools. Young Matthew's education included studies

with his father and reverend uncle and graduation from
Rugby and Oxford University. His upbringing and education exemplify the raising and teaching of the young at
their best, not so much because of social class advantages,
but that his parents and teachers sought to engage and
promote his mind and character. His rich congruence of
home and school presented no contradictions.

As an adult, Arnold enjoyed a large network of learned
friends and contacts, and his poetry and critical essays
brought him fame. His contemporary, G.W.E. Russell,
wrote in *Portraits of the Seventies* that Matthew Arnold
"was indeed the most delightful of companions, a man
of the world entirely free from worldliness and a man of
letters without the faintest trace of pedantry." Appointed
in 1857, he served as Professor of Poetry at Oxford for ten
years. He also assessed schools and their curricula all over
England as the government's Inspector of Education, a
post he held for thirty-five years. Inspecting countless
schools, Arnold attended classes and listened to the complaints of parents. Following his visitations, substandard
schools were liable to lose their government support. Also
studying school systems in France and other countries, he
presented annual reports to the government that lamented
the ill-child rearing of many caregivers and recommended
many steps to improve the schools, including increased
financial support. Very sympathetic and appreciative of
the work and difficulties of teachers, Arnold brought
about improvements in teacher training and elementary
education. He insisted that school curricula must concentrate more on mind-building literature and the humanities
than the many "useful scraps of knowledge" that schools
typically dealt with. Arnold argued that teachers should

be required to have "broader mental cultivation than was absolutely required to obtain the government certificate."

Believing that dedicated, thoughtful child rearing and education brought about a worthy people and nation, Arnold took John Donne's line, "No man is an island, entire of itself" to heart. Criticizing society and mind-set that gave little will and thought to fulfilling human potentials, he argued that a vibrant culture of people would "make the best that has been thought and known in the world current everywhere; to make all men live in an atmosphere of sweetness and light." Arnold criticized the aristocratic and educated class for its smug conceit and self-centeredness; the middle class ("Philistines") for its mercenary, "mechanical" values, and the working class for its low-mindedness and base education. Calling for "a new culture" of national revitalization, he wrote in chapter two of *Culture & Anarchy* (1861), which is still in print:

> We are still to live and grow, and this famous nation is not to stagnate and dwindle away on the one hand, or, on the other, to perish miserably in mere anarchy and confusion,—what we are on the way to. Great changes there must be, for a revolution cannot accomplish itself without great changes; yet order there must be, for without order a revolution cannot accomplish itself by due course of law.

He also repeated in several essays: "Not a having and a resting, but a growing and a becoming is the character of perfection as culture conceives it. The pursuit of perfection, then, is the pursuit of sweetness and light..." Borrowing Jonathan Swift's phrase, "sweetness and light," Arnold meant it to be the ancient Greek ideal of a perfectly well-rounded nature in people. Sweetness meant the love of beauty, both material and spiritual, and light, unbiased intelligence—the two to join and have the freest play. On the religious ethics of his times, he felt that morals and conduct were overemphasized to the neglect of New Testament love and concern for others. On democracy, he believed that political rivalry and self-interest were dangerously insufficient, that a free people should rise to scrutiny of ideas, as well as those in power, as well as to do what is good for society. On religion, he wrote poems, such as "Dover Beach" (1867), which analyzed what he saw as the problem of isolation (ignorance, self-indulgence, and depression) with the dwindling faith of his time. His many religious concerns, being a source of anxiety for him, in several essays, Arnold sought to establish the essential truth of Christianity. Arnold's upbringing and his adult intellect and commitment to values bear well on what this book is about. If America and its people are to grow and better fulfill their potentials, childcare and education must proceed in tandem, like the wheels of a bicycle.

Finally, I fantasize over what would have come about if the ten we have focused on had been switched at birth to different parents, say, Sandra O'Connor and Mae West, JFK and Hitler, and Lance Armstrong and James Conant. Because of other factors, such as genes, environment, and chance, we probably would not have Sandra dancing the shimmy, luscious Mae on the bench in judicial garb, JFK saluting Nazi style, Hitler wedded to Jackie Bouvier, and Conant cycling the Tour de France, while Lance headed Harvard and the development of the atomic bomb. Yet, it is certain that whatever the switched babies became as adults, features of their personalities and lives would be traceable to their childhoods. When I was still a boy, our family cuisine often featured delicacies, such as chicken feet and pork brain, feet, tripe, and tail. Once I asked my mother if we could have the "real" chicken and pork meat more often. Raising her eyes to the ceiling, Mom groaned, "I-yah, we got the wrong baby at the hospital!"

Other fantasies also arise from our study, such as what might have been the outcome if young Churchill had had a nanny who was the opposite of Mrs. Everest. Also, we could wonder what would have come to pass if excellent teachers, such as Robert Somervell for Churchill, Newton Henry Black for Conant, and John La Farge for James, had not influenced the boys' lives.

References

Sandra Day O'Connor:

O'Connor, Sandra Day (2005). *Chico: A true story from the childhood of the firs.* Penguin Young Readers Group.

O'Connor, Sandra Day & Day, H. Alan (2003). *Lazy B: Growing up on a cattle ranch in the American Southwest.* Random House.

Stanford Magazine articles over the years.

John F. Kennedy:

Chafe, William H. (2005). *Private lives/public consequences: Personality and politics in Modern America.* Harvard University Press.

Dallek, Robert (2003). *An unfinished life: John F. Kennedy 1917–1963*. Little, Brown.

Kennedy, Edward M. (2009). *True compass: A memoir*. Boston: Twelve Books.

Klein, Edward (2003). *The Kennedy curse: Why America's first family has neen haunted by tragedy for 150 Years*. St. Martin's Press.

Maier, Thomas (2003). *The Kennedys: America's emerald kings*. Basic.

Robert P. Hanssen:

Schiller, Lawrence (2002). *Into the mirror: The life of master spy Robert P. Hanssen.*

HarperCollins.

Shannon, Elaine & Blackman, Ann (2002). *The spy next door: The extraordinary secret life of Robert Philip Hanssen, The most damaging FBI agent in U.S. history.* Little, Brown.

Adolf Hitler:

Coetzee, J. M. (2007). "Portrait of the monster as a young artist" (review of Norman

Mailer's *The Castle in the Forest*, 2007), *The New York Review of Books*, Feb. 15, 2007, pages 8–11.

Keegan, John (1987). *The task of command*. Penguin.

Shirer, William L. (1988). *The rise and fall of Nazi Germany: A history of Nazi Germany.* Simon & Schuster.

The rise of Hitler: From unknown to dictator of Germany. The History Place. ITT Technical Institute.

Maria Augusta Trapp:

Gearin, Joan (2005). "Movie vs. reality: The real story of the von Trapp family,"37(4), National Archives, Archives.gov.

Trapp, Maria A. (1980). *The story of the Trapp Family Singers.* Perennial.

Henry James Jr.:

Edel, Leon (1996). *Henry James: A life.* Flamingo.

Richardson, Robert D. (2006). William James: *In the maelstrom of American modernism.* Houghton Mifflin.

Wills, Gary (2007). "An American hero" (review of Richardson, Robert D. (2006). *William James.* Houghton Mifflin). *New York Review of Books,* July 19, page 45.

Sir Winston Spencer Churchill:

Churchill, Randolph S. (1960). *Winston S. Churchill, Volume 1, "Youth," 1874–1900.*

Houghton Mifflin.

Churchill, Winston S. (1930). *My early life: A roving oommission.* Thornton Butterworth

Jenkins, Roy (2001). *Churchill: A biography.* Farrar, Straus and Giroux

Lance Armstrong:

Coyle, Daniel (2005). *Lance Armstrong's war.* HarperCollins.

Media coverage of his Tour de France races

Mae West:

Watts, Jill (2001). *Mae West: An icon in black and white.* Oxford University

James Bryant Conant:

Hershberg, James G. (1993). *James B. Conant: Harvard to Hiroshima and the making of the nuclear age.* Alfred A. Knopf.

CHAPTER SIX

AMERICA'S FLAWED EDUCATIONAL SYSTEM

While critics tend to rely on the three-decades long decline of the Scholastic Aptitude Test (SAT) to document the dumbing down of American education, more alarming is our performance against the students of other industrialized countries. By virtually every measure of achievement, American students lag far behind their counterparts in both Asia and Europe, especially in math and science.

—Charles J. Sykes, *Dumbing down our kids: Why America's children feel good about themselves but can't read, write, or add.* 1996

This chapter relates to the educational concerns of many Americans, including presidents. A Department of Education report on education in the U.S. was released during President Ronald Reagan's presidency in 1983 with the title, "A Nation at Risk." The commission that produced it included eighteen prominent persons from the private sector, government, and education. Their report contained shockingly bold statements, such as, "the educational foundations of our society are presently being eroded by a rising tide of mediocrity that threatens our very future as a Nation and a people," and "If an unfriendly foreign power had attempted to impose on America the mediocre educational performance that exists today, we might well have viewed it as an act of war." Following a national stir over the report, few if any improvements materialized.

In early colonial days, settlers hired slightly educated, itinerant teachers to live in their homes awhile to teach children the three-Rs, mainly so that the kids could learn enough to read the Bible. Education expanded in the nineteenth century, when one-room schools began to be established by localities throughout the predominantly rustic nation. Like Abe Lincoln, children walked miles to school. At first, schoolmarms, who were under-educated, poorly paid, and likely to marry one of the older boys in her school, taught the many thousands of one-room schools. States gradually established two-year normal schools to train eighth-grade graduates to become primary school teachers after the State of Massachusetts opened the first in Lexington in 1839. It has evolved into today's Framingham State College, which provides general curricula, as well as teacher training. Educational reformers in the nineteenth century, such as Horace Mann and James G. Carter, led the fight for public education and teacher training. Many public universities today first started as normal schools, such as San Francisco State, as mentioned in chapter four. As high schools developed, states expanded normal schools into four-year institutions. Teacher education was practical instead of classical higher learning as taught at four-year universities, the reason for the term "normal." Revealing the provincialism of our educational system, several teachers I taught with told me that when they started to teach, they had to sign contracts that said they would lose their jobs if they ever married.

Although one-room schools are scarce today, they are recalled with nostalgia—their rustic settings, wood stoves, characteristic architecture, outhouses, bell-ringing calls to attend class, and community/religious meetings. If they could afford the tuition, parents sent their children to private schools in the cities. Therefore, the one-room school system and normal schools set in motion much of America's pattern for public education. As this chapter examines defects of the nation's educational system and teacher training, improvements will be discussed.

In a thoughtful article, Andrew Delbanco wrote that Americans have criticized and debated over their country's educational programs and system for 150 years. Prophesying that if moderating compromise doesn't develop in the polarized battles over education, he said:

> Otherwise we will remain caught between the usual warring parties: pro-teacher-union versus anti-union groups; those who favor mayoral control against those who prefer community control; devotees of phonics versus "whole language" theorists; "open classroom" versus fixed-seat advocates; those who believe in "pull-out" groups versus those who believe in whole-class learning; those who believe that tests motivate academic improvements versus those who think tests hold teacher unfairly accountable and create a climate of fear; those who think the formative period is early childhood against those who are sure it is adolescence; those who see private initiatives like Teach for America (TFA)—which recruits teachers straight out of liberal arts colleges—as an answer to

teacher burnout against those who think TFA gives
municipalities an excuse to cut school budgets.

There are more disputes, such as dress codes, teaching
evolution as science, intelligent design, or creationism,
and differing approaches to sex education. However, concentrating on domestic clashes, Delbanco doesn't mention what I believe tops the list—results of international
tests that consistently disgrace the schooling and achievement of U.S. students. The public is either unaware of the
miserable disaster or hasn't taken it seriously, even though
they are equivalent to the catastrophes of Pearl Harbor
and 9/11 that greatly endangered the U.S.

The Organisation for Economic Co-operation and
Development's (OECD) periodic report in 2009, *Doing
Better for Children*, found that American 15–16-year-olds
ranked 21st out of 30 nations in science and 25th out of 30
in math–far below leading Finland but above Mexico at
the very bottom. The OECD reported that while the U.S.
spends more per child than most nations U.S. educational
and health results are among the very worst. That means
funding by the states and Washington is not consistent
and well-coordinated.

Newsweek magazine's (August 16, 2010) rankings of
100 worldwide nations ranked America 26th in education,
26th in health, 9th in quality of life, 2nd in economic dyna-
mism, and 14th in political environment. Finland ranked
tops in education with Canada and South Korea tied for
second, Singapore 4th, and Japan 5th. Just ahead of the U.S.
was Latvia in 25th place and Hungary, 24th.

The UNICEF's 2007 report on children's well-being
in twenty-one rich nations rated America at the very bot-

tom with Britain. The report raised the outcry of child-care, education, welfare, and pediatrician groups in both nations, especially in Great Britain, which has close ties to UNICEF. Blame was heaped on America's and Britain's social and economic systems, as the report said that both societies have gone from relatively equal societies after the Depression and World War II, to become the most unequal in wealth and social condition among all rich nations. While other developed countries deliberately seek social equality and provide generous social assistance to the poor and unemployed and families with children, America and Britain provide much less in comparison, and what is available is ineffective to break the poor's cycle of poverty. The reader can see that significant improvements in education would involve big societal changes, as first discussed in chapter one.

OECD's, UNICEF's and *Newsweek's* findings are reflected in the night and day differences in how America conducts its educational system versus nations with superior student achievement. In 2007, McKinsey & Co., a highly respected New York consultancy firm that has served many governments and companies, released a well-documented report authored by Michael Barber and Mona Mourshed, "How the World's Best Performing Schools Systems Come Out on Top." Journeying worldwide to find what worked or not, the McKinsey researchers concluded that the countries with the best student achievement and teaching effectiveness were Canada, Finland, Japan, Singapore, and South Korea. The report's opening paragraph highlighted their strengths:

> The top-performing school systems consistently attract more able people into the teaching profession, leading to better student outcomes. They do this by making entry to teacher training highly selective, developing effective processes for selecting the right applicants to become teachers, and paying good (but not great) starting compensation. Getting these essentials right drives up the status of the profession, enabling it to attract even better candidates.

The key to the success of the world's top-performing school systems is that they are efficiently administered and financed by their national governments. In comparison, instead of a coordinated, national educational system, America has a desultory patchwork of almost 15,000 school districts. Because public education in America is the purview of the states and localities, the policies, management, funding, and the size of school systems are uneven and varied. Many school districts are so small that one building is sufficient for all of their students and teachers, while some are so huge, as Los Angeles and New York, that they count schools in the thousands. I began teaching in a country school with three teachers and classrooms where I taught grades four, five, and six. Just imagine how it would be if America's national defense was handled by the fifty states and localities instead of the federal government. Addressing the problems spelled out by the "A Nation at Risk" report, President Reagan recommended greater choice and availability in which schools youngsters attend, including subsidized private schools. Today's charter schools probably stem from that.

Because the Tenth Amendment of the Constitution gives the states the responsibility and authority for all functions not delegated to the federal government, education is the prerogative of the fifty states. Each state regulates its own educational policies and certifies educators' qualifications. Each state assigns local boards of education the responsibility to manage public education, raise property taxes to fund their schools, and employ teachers and administrators. Unless one unified district has been formed, independent boards manage different grade levels, such as K-6, 8–12, and community colleges (13–14). Some states put community colleges under the control of the university board. To complicate the management situation further, county governments are also involved. Each state funds public higher education within its borders and assigns authority to a board of regents. Contributing about 8 percent of the total educational costs, federal support has come through special laws, as in Head Start, promoting integration, assisting the handicapped, and special programs, such as the Elementary and Secondary Act (1965) and the "No Child Left Behind" law (2001).

Unlike America's splintered system of education, central governments of foreign nations, such as Finland and Singapore, with their outstanding student achievement and well-trained teachers, administer and finance their national educational systems. All of their educators are employees of the national government and curriculum is uniform nationwide. Because national governments wield far greater authority and funding power than provincial and grassroots government levels, education in top-performing countries lacks America's mishmash problems.

American teachers are not well paid. Because of that fact and the relative ease to become a teacher, the standing of educators is not nearly what it should be. Exposing a contradiction between intent and reality, Americans insist that their children should receive the best education, yet they will vote down taxes to raise teachers' salaries and they give little attention to school board elections. Circumspect on the boast that public schools are governed democratically at the grass roots, it is not uncommon for school board members to seek and assume office with weak credentials and axes to grind, such as dedication to cut school taxes and further or hinder the teaching of controversial topics. Schools across the country are old and in serious disrepair because of neglect. In many states, first-year teachers receive pay that borders the poverty level. Senior teachers earn salaries that put them in the middle class, but their pay is far lower than new MBA graduates. In short, America's system of public education is not conducive to uniform, first-rate professionalism and efficiency.

Convinced that quality education relies on superior teaching, foreign nations with the best student achievement concentrate very hard on teacher selection and training. Before university students in Finland, Singapore, and South Korea are selected to enter teacher education, they are carefully screened on their past academic achievement, communication skills, and motivation for teaching. This is most unlike America, where students who want to be teachers enroll with no screening in state-approved university programs, which when completed, they are accredited to teach. With SAT and other aptitude scores at the bottom level of university students, elementary education students even join other students in chastising their coursework as "Mickey Mouse," e.g., easy and meaningless. Those seeking to be secondary teachers embrace their subject matter courses and look down on their education studies.

Improving education is a top priority of the Obama administration. In October 2009, Arne Duncan, U.S. Secretary of Education, called for a "revolutionary" overhaul of America's "mediocre" teacher education programs and certification policies. His Columbia University speech denounced universities for shortchanging quality preparation of teachers by using the high enrollments of schools of education as "cash cows" in order to fund academic programs and staff with more prestige. As a former dean of education myself, I can verify what Secretary Duncan said. With budgets for my school of education requiring the highest enrollments of the university, my faculty had to teach double and more students and courses than any other school of the university. I also agree with Duncan when he also said that education professors tend to be decades behind the times and steeped in theory that isn't useful in classrooms. He announced that the Obama administration will fund outstanding teacher-training programs and boost them as examples for others. One example he praised was that Louisiana traces tests scores of fourth- to ninth-graders back to their teachers, and from there, to where the teachers received their training for certification. State teacher education schools are then instructed to improve if needed.

Announcing the "Race to the Top" educational reform initiative with President Obama in July 2009, Duncan said he will emphasize more accountability and higher standards with $4.35 billion from the stimulus funds of American Recovery and Reinvestment Act. The goals of the initiative are:

1)   adoption of college- and career-ready
      standards and assessments;

2)   recruitment, development, rewarding, and
      retaining effective teachers and principals;

3)   building data systems that measure stu-
      dent success and inform teachers and
      principals about how they can improve
      their practices; and

4)   turning around low-performing schools.

In March 2010, out of sixteen states competing for "Race
to the Top" grants, Tennessee was awarded $500 million
and Delaware $100 million by the U.S. Education Depart-
ment. Its complex scoring system weighted everything
from the states' willingness to track student and teacher
performance, adopt uniform standards, and turn around
or close their worst schools. To compete at all, states seeking funds must have adopted the Common Core State
Standards, which more than thirty have adopted in late
2010. Delaware had proposed an overhaul plan that will
identify the state's worst-performing schools and then
turn them around within two years. It also gained high
marks for pledging to grant extra bonuses to teachers and
principals willing to work in the toughest, academically-
challenged schools. Tennessee lawmakers passed new
education laws to lift its cap on the number of new charter schools, which are schools that are taxpayer funded,
but are independently run. Both states have imposed
new measures that teacher pay and promotions are partly
based on how well their students perform. Competition
for "Race to the Top" grants will continue.

To improve math and English language achievement, in March 2010 the National Governors Association and the Council of Chief State School Officers issued an impressive recommendation to the states that they called Common Core State Standards. CCSS is a grade-by-grade list of standards of what students should be taught and what they should be expected to achieve, and was painstakingly drafted by teachers, mathematicians, statisticians, mathematic educators, and cognitive scientists with input from educational groups. Proposing a coherent curricular strategy and standards, CCSS stresses math and language achievement and ends the mishmash manner in which the subjects are taught across America with uniform structure and proficiency. For example, fewer topics at each grade level are to be taught but each to greater depth, as in countries with high achieving students. As topics are covered at appropriate grade levels, teachers and youths build on solid grounding–from what students know to the unknown. Textbooks and student assessment within and across states would be improved. A meaningful curriculum strategy makes great sense and states and schools should implement CCSS' ideas. Good teachers are essential, and their effectiveness requires stepwise, grade-by-grade curricular, syllabus strategy and standards that build new knowledge and skills on what had been learned.

Seeking to improve science and math education for middle and high school students, in January 2010 the White House has also mounted an after-school campaign it calls "Educate to Innovate," with the volunteer support of individuals and nonprofit groups and companies, such as the Science Channel; John D. and Catherine T. MacArthur Foundation; PBS' *Sesame Street*; Sally K. Ride, the first

American woman in space; Craig R. Barrett, former chairman of Intel; Ursula M. Burns, Xerox CEO; and Time Warner Cable's CEO, Glenn A. Britt. The purpose of the "Educate to Innovate" campaign is to encourage students to study math, technology, science, and engineering with stimulating scientific programs and games.

In nations with outstanding educational systems, students who seek university admission must pass stiff entrance examinations. As I found through research on higher education in Asia (e.g., *East Asian Higher Education: Traditions and Transformations*) tough entrance exams are generally the rule worldwide for university admissions. America is exceptional in that students who are ineligible for prestigious universities can enroll at universities with less demanding admission standards, and community colleges, which accept almost anyone. Those wanting to be primary school teachers in South Korea must score in the top five percent on university entrance exams before they can be selected to undergo a demanding course of study in teacher institutions. The competition to teach in the early grades, which I regard as the most important school years, helps to assure that teachers are not only intelligent, motivated, and caring, but also tops academically. Thus, South Korean primary teachers have very high social status, even higher than secondary teachers, whose selection and training are not as rigorous, because their subject-matter knowledge is regarded as most vital to their teaching. Besides careful pre-screening of aspiring teachers, high-performing nations limit the number of students accepted for teacher training to available school openings, again unlike the U.S. Those selected for teacher training in South Korea receive personalized guidance and ongoing evaluations to identify and eliminate weak trainees. Weeding of American teacher candidates rarely occurs.

Leading nations in UNICEF's report pay high salaries to school principals, who rise from the teaching ranks on the basis of their instructional leadership skills. They pay starting teachers well, but not extravagantly, averaging 95–99 percent of GDP per capita, meaning the nation's median salary. South Korea affords the most with 141 percent of GDP per capita, which with America's GDP per capita of $ 46,381 in 2009 would translate to $65,397. Other well-performing countries start new teachers with salaries at their national income medians, which is highly superior to the subsistence-level pay that's paid U.S. first-year teachers. The McKinsey & Co. report said,

> A good salary is not necessarily the main or only motivation for teaching, of course. Surveys show that most people who enter the teaching profession do so for a range of reasons, the foremost of which is the desire to help a new generation succeed ... However, the surveys also show that unless school systems offer salaries which are in-line with other graduates' starting salaries, these same people do not enter teaching.

Nations with the best teacher salaries, Britain, Germany, Spain, and Switzerland, have not improved educational outcomes. Thus, while good pay draws outstanding persons into teaching, much more is needed, chiefly diligent screening and training of teachers.

What high-performing nations do in teacher training can also succeed in America. The public school district of Chicago, where Arne Duncan served as school superintendent before President Obama appointed him to be Secretary of Education, strongly embraces the idea that quality education comes from quality instruction. Believing the same, Boston's school district pays the highest starting salaries in Massachusetts. With its Teach First and Teach for America programs, Boston's deliberate attention on raising attitudes toward teaching to the level of high-status professions has increased the number of talented and capable people recruited to teaching. Chicago's Teaching Fellows and Boston's Teaching Residency programs, which screen and train a limited number of new teachers, attract the same high caliber of candidates as in Singapore and other leading nations. As McKinsey & Co. reported:

> Boston has introduced a graduate teacher training program based on a medical-residency model, combining a large amount of practical experience, a strong theoretical background, and a higher-level (masters) degree qualification. After an initial six-week summer school, trainee teachers spend one year on an appren-ticeship in schools. During this year they spend four days each week working with an experienced teacher, and one day a week doing coursework. During their second year, each new teacher is allocated a mentor who provides two-and-a-half hours of in-class coaching each week. Mentors model, co-teach, observe and help with classroom management, lesson planning and instructional strategies. In order to improve the quality of mentoring on the program, Boston now employs a number of full-time specialist mentors, each of whom supports 14 new teachers.

"Children's Chances
Vary Across States"

The Editorial Projects in Education deserves great credit for producing the data and charts that follow, and I praise *Education Week* for publishing their superb report January 4, 2007, titled, "Quality Counts 2007: From Cradle to Career." The fifty states and the District of Columbia were compared with scores on thirteen indexes. Shedding glaring light on America's educational system, it exposed shocking differences between states. Let's highlight the best and worst states to understand just what creates such differences—Virginia (1st) earned the highest "Chance-for-Success" in life score in preparing children for their futures, and New Mexico (51st) had the lowest score. In the following chart, the versus given with Virginia's (VA) percentage scores are the national readings, as in the first, Family Income, VA has 69.7% for children from families with incomes at least 200 percent of poverty level, as versus or compared to 59.8% nationally. Of course, the national percentage of 59.8% is the same for New Mexico (NM), e.g., 44.7% vs. 59.8%. Note that NM lags both VA and the national percentage in all indexes.

A.	Family Income	Parent Education	Parental Employment
	(% children from families w/incomes at least 200% of poverty level)	(% of children with at least one parent w/college degree)	(% of children w/at least one parent working full time and year-round)
Virginia	69.7% vs. U.S. 59.8%	50.6% vs. U.S. 42.5%	76.2% vs. U.S. 70.6%
New Mexico	44.7%	33.6%	65.4%

B.	Linguistic Integration	Preschool Enrollment	Kindergarten Enrollment
	(% of children whose parents are fluent English speakers)	(% of 3- and 4-year olds enrolled in preschool)	(% of eligible children enrolled in K.)
Virginia	90.5% vs. 84.3%	46.5% vs. 44.8%	74.3% vs. 75.3%
New Mexico	79.7%	39.2%	74.3%

C.	Elmentary Reading	Middle School Math	High School Graduation
	(% of 4th Grade public school pupils "proficient"	(% of public school 8th Graders "proficient")	(% public school HS students ho graduate with diplomas)
Virginia	36.9% vs. 29.8%	33.4% vs. 28.5%	74.9% vs. 69.6%
New Mexico	20.5%	14.0%	56.7%

D.	Postsecondary Participation	College Attainment	Annual Income
	(% of young adults, 18-24, enrolled in college or with a degree)	% of adults, 25-64, with a 2- or 4-year degree	% of adults, 25-64, with incomes at or above U.S. Median
Virginia	50.2% vs. 47.8%	42.6% vs. 37.4%%	56.6% vs. 50.0%
New Mexico	38.9%	33.5%	42.5%

E.	Steady Employment		
	(% of adults, 24-64, working full time and year-round)		
Virginia	72.% vs. 67.2%	New Mexico	64.2%

Taking the six indexes on lines A and B as family readiness to support children's learning aptitude (excepting data for kindergarten enrollment, since both VA and NM afford public kindergartens), we see that NM kids are severely shortchanged as compared to kids in VA. While parents' employment in NM is lower, but not overly amiss from the national average and that of VA, jobs in NM and VA are far from equivalent, given the differences in parents' income and education. The VA-NM contrast shows how family and school factors can affect kids' lives, but we need to know much more. Some information usually leads to more questions.

The following map shows how children's life prospects vary greatly from state to state. While children in New Mexico have the lowest "Chance-for-Success" in life scores, the map shows that there are many other states that also present poor life prospects for kids, as shown on the map in white—Alabama, Arizona, Louisiana, Mississippi, Nevada, Tennessee, Texas, and West Virginia. Children in states with excellent "Chance-for-Success" scores are fortunate indeed—Connecticut, Delaware, Minnesota, Nebraska, New Hampshire, Rhode Island, Vermont, Virginia, and Wisconsin as shown on the map in black. A regional effect appears to be working in that low-scoring states are in the southern Sun Belt, and high scorers are in the Northeast.

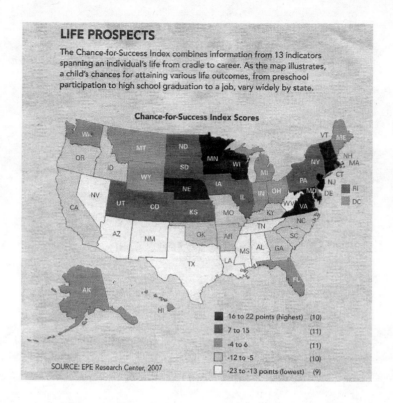

LIFE PROSPECTS

The Chance-for-Success Index combines information from 13 indicators spanning an individual's life from cradle to career. As the map illustrates, a child's chances for attaining various life outcomes, from preschool participation to high school graduation to a job, vary widely by state.

Chance-for-Success Index Scores

- 16 to 22 points (highest) (10)
- 7 to 15 (11)
- -4 to 6 (11)
- -12 to -5 (10)
- -23 to -13 points (lowest) (9)

SOURCE: EPE Research Center, 2007

The next chart compares five states on *Education Week*'s fourteen indexes. Differences are stark at the far right end with Virginia leading at the top, Wyoming, Ohio, and California in the middle, and New Mexico at the bottom. The lower part of the chart outlines the fourteen indexes, with each of the five states beginning exactly at the same point when children are newborns and infants. From that equal start, the five states diverge from left to right, beginning with Family Income and ending with the index of Steady Employment.

DIVERGENT PATHS

States gain or lose points on each Chance-for-Success indicator based on how they perform compared with the national average. Putting that picture together across each of the 13 indicators, selected to represent critical life junctures, reveals a state's educational trajectory from childhood through adulthood. As the graph below illustrates, where you live matters. A child born in Virginia has a better-than-average chance for success at every stage, while a child from New Mexico is likely to face a series of hurdles throughout life.

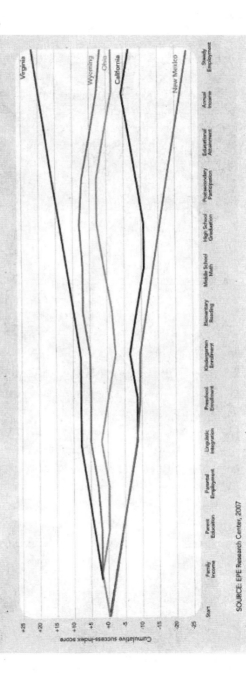

SOURCE: EPE Research Center, 2007

It is interesting to note that California and New Mexico parallel each other from the start through Linguistic Integration, which large Latino populations in both states probably account for. Once America's educational leader, California has fallen tremendously in K-12 educational quality ever since Proposition 13's property tax revolt of 1978 drastically cut school funds. The rural, small-populated state of Wyoming does fairly well until Postsecondary Participation, Educational Attainment, Annual Income, and Steady Employment kick in.

More Specific Data is Needed

When their children are seriously hurt and sick, families seek medical assistance without delay. Yet delegating children's learning and mental development wholly to schools, and doing little or nothing at home and elsewhere is the same as ignoring their health. The chart just displayed supposedly shows how its listed indexes influence youths' chances in life for better or worse. However, the most crucial indexes in my thinking are not represented, which I believe should comprise the learning climate of homes, schools, and neighborhood and community resources. Without that data, are we to assume that parents' income, employment, education, etc., are sufficient to explain why Virginia stands highest in the nation for children's life prospects and New Mexico the lowest? Parents' income, employment, etc., are valuable socioeconomic data, but we need indexes that go more specifically to children's development that prepare them for their tomorrows.

Displaying an ever-widening gap from left to right between Virginia and New Mexico, the chart's indexes of High School Graduation, Postsecondary Participation,

and Educational Attainment lead to or predict the con-
cluding indexes of Annual Income and Steady Employment, or simply, less education means less pay and jobs.
If we had indexes on learning climate to the left of the
chart when children are young, they would be more helpful in predicting High School Graduation, etc. Since this
book discusses children's early years as the most important
of their lives, we must have earlier predictors of progress
than High School Graduation when youths' life chances
are already well set. We need to stem VA/NM-like contrasts as early as possible by raising the learning climate
of low performing states. The differences among states
could be lessened when learning and attitudes are boosted
through deliberate, collective effort. Costs could be less
than supposed.

Therefore, to gauge learning climate, additional
indexes that I would include in the chart are:

1) Family reading and study habits of adults
and children;

2) Hours of children's daily TV viewing
(reverse scoring, i.e., few or none to be
rewarded);

3) Teachers' salaries;

4) Teachers' education and training;

5) Availability of communities' library and
museum resources;

6) Children's use of No. 5 resources;

7) Neighborhood study groups, if any.

How would states compare on those seven indexes? My indexes would highlight where and how every state, especially the lesser scoring ones, could improve their climate of learning and standing. With greater foresight, VA and NM could see how they could improve their curves.

Organizing Schools for Improvement:

Lessons from Chicago, a praiseworthy book by Anthony S. Bryk and others of the Consortium on Chicago School Research zeroed in on severely disadvantaged neighborhoods and their schools. Supporting what I have just said about focusing on indexes of learning climate early on, it said that the way to turn hard-to-improve schools around is to mount an "integrated set of community, school, and related social-service programs." Also, as *edweek.org* reported on January 25, 2010, the Bryk book reported five ingredients of quality schools:

1) "Strong leadership, in the sense that principals are 'strategic,' focused on instruction, and inclusive of others in the work;

2) "A welcoming attitude toward parents, and formation of connections with the community;

3) "Development of professional capacity, which refers to the quality of the teaching staff, teachers' belief that schools can change, and participation in good professional development and collaborative work;"

4) "A learning climate that is safe, welcoming, stimulating, and nurturing to all students; and

5) "Strong instructional guidance and materials."

Research by Robert Crosnoe and others is supportive of (4) and (5). Researching different environmental (social) settings and how they affected young children's math and reading achievement, they found that positive cognitive stimulation that's provided at three crucial points—home, child care, and first grade, promoted good achievement, especially for low-income kids.

Psychologists have found that although the learning readiness and aptitude of youths advance satisfactorily through elementary school, steady state typically comes in secondary school. In their late teens, people reach their life plateaus in aptitude and IQ tests and progress little further. Of course, little kids dashing off to kindergarten and primary school know little and eagerly soak up what they learn. While moving from standstill indicates progress, it is difficult to maintain steady progress with poor learning readiness and awareness. Comparing where kids were at first-grade to their growth by sixth-grade can be wondrous to see. For, in six years, most normal twelve-year-olds can read and figure as well as average adults and have grown physically too. But can they spiral up further from there? As discussed at the start of this book, infants are genetically programmed with readiness to learn rudiments of their caregivers' language. By the time they are teenagers, they have gained knowledge and formed learning skills and attitudes, but the big questions about their futures are: Were they taught so well in their early years at school and home that their learning and thinking continued to spiral as teenagers? Are they outstanding or just average secondary students? Will they go on to higher education and where? What livelihoods will they qualify for and seek?

Parents who rest assured that their kids' bright progress through the primary grades foretells further success in higher grades should think again—good, youthful learning is generally par and should be expected for most. Instead of continuous mental growth, however, except for exceptions, the mental power of the vast majority of post-teen adults plateaus before they are nineteen, probably earlier for the severely disadvantaged. Doing better than that is quite possible if children are raised and taught properly during their earliest years. What this book discusses and recommends can make all the difference in youths' progress in mind and character, and the nature of their tomorrows.

In Closing

This book has answered the six questions raised on its first page. Children begin to learn as soon as they are born. The period of life that is most determining of an individual's future is childhood. Teachers are vital, but parents and relatives have much greater opportunity to teach and influence children. Positive attachment and social interaction are the most crucial factors in parenting and teaching. The one right way to raise, teach, and discipline children is with the authoritative-engaging style. Good character, learning readiness and awareness arise from those factors, and, of course, the children's tomorrows. Finally, America's K-12 educational system is one of the worst among the world's developed nations. It's an excuse-prone, inefficient system—a pathetic "broken window" to use Michael Levine's term, which harms national progress and U.S. preeminence as world leader. Contradicting the country's democratic principles of equality and the pursuit of happiness, its defects include expanding and solidifying the divide between those who have and those who are disadvantaged. Universally regarded as the world's best, its elite universities and military academies have long provided the nation with many of its talented and well-educated leaders and professionals, which in coming decades may not be sufficient to maintain America's prominence as other nations advance with outstanding K-12 and higher education programs.

Demonstrating inspired dedication to teaching, I recommend the film, *The Hobart Shakespeareans*, to educators and parents. It is about Rafe Esquith, a 5th-grade teacher who promotes poor, immigrant children's learning and preparation for life at Hobart Boulevard Elementary School in Los Angeles with an enrollment of 2,000. His books, such as *Teach Like Your Hair's on Fire*, should be read by aspiring teachers. Esquith's efforts have been broadly acclaimed, by groups such as *Parents Magazine* and Oprah Winfrey's $100,000 "Use Your Life Award." the National Medal of the Arts in 2003, the only teacher so honored by the White House. I would like to meet and compare notes with Esquith, and many others cited in this book.

As Rafe works each day including weekends from dawn to evening with the backing of many supporters, few teachers do what he does. A surprising caveat arose in the film when his principal said that Hobart's teachers disliked him. We get a clue why they dislike him from a 2007 interview when Rafe complained, "I have still not been to one staff meeting where character was discussed, honestly discussed—how we get children to behave themselves, not because they're afraid of punishment but because they really adopt a code of civil behavior." It would be interesting to know how Hobart School's 6th-grade teachers react to and manage the pupils that Esquith taught and what adjustments the kids make. If reasons for his peers' disfavor include feeling envious or belittled by all he does, the question can be raised, What can teachers accomplish by teaching a normal schedule of

8 to 3, five workdays compared to Esquith's all-consuming efforts? My classroom work (chapter four), which was very rewarding, involved afterhours and weekends but nothing like Esquith's tireless efforts. However, though their home life was mostly mean and destitute, my Windsor School kids spoke English and were born Americans, unlike his Korean and Central American immigrants. The critical factors in outstanding teaching come from MAC (mutually assured connectivity) attachment and social interaction with youths, sound curricular strategy and standards to work with, determination, and professional knowhow and intelligence to do the best possible. How many teachers have we had that made ill use of time, and did we need our best teachers to be with us night and day? Yet, it's because Esquith's pupils present tremendous challenges in language and other disadvantages that he does everything he can to boost their motivation, awareness, and learning readiness in just one school year. Since many of his former students are now university graduates and most are doing well, his example shows what it takes to redirect severe student handicaps for the good.

Because America's state by state educational system is a conglomeration and its teacher-training programs are deficient, the nation pales in comparison with leading nations in educating children, quality selection of and training teachers, and providing social assistance to needy families. High-performing nations in education, such as Finland, have more homogeneous and smaller populations than the U.S. and are not burdened by massive defense budgets. America spends more on defense ($720 billion for fiscal year 2011, up from 663.8 b. for FY 2010, about 19% of the federal budget) than on education (about

$638 billion per year and declining as states and localities are forced to cut budgets). In comparison, Canada spends 6.3% of its federal budget on defense and 12.7% on education. It costs the U.S. from $250,000 to one million a year for each American soldier in Iraq and Afghanistan. In August 2010, U.S. Defense Secretary Robert Gates said that he was cutting $100 billion from the defense budget.

So that our children can have the fullest success and happiness through their entire lives, we must stop wasting their early years out of the mistaken belief that they aren't capable of much learning and that learning is a chore. In that wondrous moment when newborns breathe for the very first time, they are most extraordinary beings with inborn mental and physical potentials that can proliferate in growth over the years under the right conditions. Abundant possibilities lie before them if they are properly raised and taught. Increasingly, know-how and mental abilities are today and will continue to be in demand and rewarded.

The human brain evolved to facilitate learning, reasoning, memory, and the ability to cope and search for meaning. If children receive positive home, school, and civic conditions as this book discusses, their effectiveness, morality, and decency as good citizens will blossom and mature in adulthood. Since children can't choose their parents, it's a fortunate child that goes to loving, authoritative-engaging parents with smarts. The United States of America will flourish anew as more and more enlightened parents raise their children properly, school systems foster coherent curricular strategy and standards and hire and retain only the most able teachers, and community resources promote favorable learning climates. Since the states' prerogative in public education will not change, greater federal involvement in education is essential. Greater heed must be given to the recommendations of child-oriented research groups, such as the National Scientific Council on the Developing Child. A provocative line I read still haunts me. It said that American children are the happiest and most physically fit in the world, but they are among the developed nations' lowest in schooling and cognitive development.

To conclude the book, let me tell an anecdote. In 1966, I was invited to a select research conference at the famed Grossinger's ski resort in New York's Catskills Mountains. Following another of the scrupulous dinners that featured platters of delicious steaks, I wandered into the lounge. There I found a group of mothers with their young children and a comedian. As I sat down, the comedian was teasing the ladies, "Oh, I know what you're doing—calling that child doctor, that one attorney, and over there the professor. Yes, I know how you're raising those kids."

INDEX AND NOTES

behavior." *Genetic Psychology Monographs*, 75(1), 43–88 and (1978). "Parental disciplinary patterns and social competence in children." *Youth and Society*, 9, 238–276; **43**

Bergeson, Terry; Washington State Superintendent of Public Education, 1996–2008, **87**

bilingualism; **22**; childhood is the ideal time of life to learn more than one language. As discussed in chapter one, proper language development of the young must be taken seriously. Family verbiage with a mix of words from different languages does not produce bilingualism. What children hear and speak becomes their primary language. Because of the illiterate and superficial language many children are exposed to in households, their developing a sound foundation in English is hampered and bilingualism is out of the question.

Lasting, true bilingualism is when people have separate, self-contained language structures imbedded in their memory. To develop that with the young, have one parent speak only one language, such as English, in the presence of a child and another parent speak another language whenever the child is present and speaking to each parent in the language he or she speaks. Or on consistent alternate days both parents speak only one language and on other days speak another language with the child following suit. Relatives can serve as second-language speakers if they only speak the second language and spend time with the child and speak widely on topics. That's the same for kids interacting with natives In foreign lands for extensive time. That's how children can begin to form distinct, cognitive language structures. That is the audio-lingual approach used by the best foreign language training institutes, and is far superior to the way foreign language teachers have taught through translations from and to English, such as learning Spanish, say, by translating English into Spanish equivalents and from Spanish back to English. That superimposes Spanish onto the English structure, which gets lost by lack of practice and the dominant use of English. Also, translations cannot cover the true, cultural sense of foreign words and ideas.

Those who learn a foreign language vicariously when they are adults can rarely speak with native quality, because of the fixed dominance of their primary language. Children's education is hampered at school by families that speak a foreign language and little or no English. Special pre-school programs should be established to aid such children.

covered the double helix structure of DNA; the three awarded the 1962 Nobel Prize for Physiology or Medicine, **144**

Crisp, Quentin (1908–1999); author of *The Naked Civil Servant*, **197**

Crosnoe, Robert and others, (2010). "Family socioeconomic status and consistent environmental stimulation in early childhood." *Child Development*, 81(3), 972–987; **236-237**

Cunha, Flavio; Assistant Professor of Economics, University of Pennsylvania; first author with James J. Heckman (2008). "Formulating, Identifying and estimating the technology of cognitive and noncognitive skill formation," *Journal of Human Resources*, 43(4), 738–782; **22-23**

curricular strategy and standards, **23, 225, 241, 242**

Daily Star newspaper of Bangladesh, **20**

Daoism or Taoism, depending on pronunciation; the Dao meaning The Way, which one must seek to obtain natural goodness. Millennia-old Chinese philosophy and for many a religion that stress the Three Jewels of the Dao - compassion, moderation, and humility. Lao Zi (sixth century BCE) founded the Daoist movement by writing *Dao De Jing* (Power and Principle - "to know the invariable is enlightenment." "Daoism focuses on change and nature and their universality and harmony, humans being just one element of the cosmos. Health and lon-

Canada, and internationally; publishes the *Journal for Research in Mathematics Education, Teaching Children Mathematics, Mathematics Teaching in the Middle School,* and *Mathematics Teacher,* **86-87**

National Institute for Early Education Research (NIEER); "conducts and communicates research to support high quality, effective, early childhood education for all young children;" **33-34**

National Medal of the Arts; annual award created by Congress in 1984 to honor artists and patrons of the arts. Honorees are selected by the National Endowment for the Arts and ceremoniously presented by the President. The 2009 awardees were Bob Dylan, singer-songwriter; Clint Eastwood, actor and director; Milton Glaser, graphic designer; Maya Lin, artist and architect; Rita Moreno, singer and actor; Jessye Norman, soprano; Joseph P. Riley, Jr., mayor of Charleston, South Carolina; Frank Stella, artist; Michael Tilson Thomas, conductor; John Williams, composer; the Oberlin Conservatory of Music; and the School of American Ballet, **240**

National Scientific Council on the Developing Child; a multidisciplinary collaboration of scientists and scholars from universities across the United States and Canada designed to bring the science of early childhood and early brain development to bear on public policy decision-making; "flagship initiative on translating science into policy" of Harvard University's Center on the Developing Child; sample of NSCDC reports: "A Science-Based Framework for Early Childhood Policy," Center for the Developing Child, Harvard University, 2007; "The Science of Early Childhood Development: What We Know and What We Do," Center for the Developing Child, Harvard University, 2007; **22, 243**

Nave, Christopher; PhD candidate at the University of California, Riverside; personality study accepted for publication by the journal, *Social Psychological and Personality Science*, with the title, "On the contextual independence of personality: Teachers' assessments predict directly observed behavior after four decades." Co-authors are Professors Ryne A. Sherman, David C. Funder, Sarah E. Hampson, and Lewis R. Goldberg, **22** From *Science Daily's* digest of Nave's study:

1) Youngsters identified as verbally fluent—defined as unrestrained talkativeness—tended, as middle-aged adults, to display interest in intellectual matters, speak fluently, try to control the situation, and exhibit a high degree of intelligence. Children rated low in verbal fluency by their teachers were observed as adults to seek advice, give up when faced with obstacles, and exhibit an awkward interpersonal style.

2) Children rated as highly adaptable—defined as coping easily and successfully with new situations—tended, as middle-aged adults, to behave cheerfully, speak fluently and show interest in intellectual matters. Those who rated low in adaptability as children were observed as adults to say negative things about themselves, seek advice and exhibit an awkward interpersonal style.

3) Students rated as impulsive as adults were inclined to speak   loudly, display a wide range of interests and be talkative. Those who were rated low on impulsivity were observed, as adults, to be fearful or timid, keep others at a distance and express insecurity.

4) Children whose teachers rated them as having a tendency to self-minimize—defined as humble, minimizing their own importance or never show-ing off—as adults were likely to express guilt, seek reassurance, say negative things about themselves and express in-security. Those who were ranked low as self-minimizing were observed as adults to speak loudly, show interest in intellectual matters and exhibit condescending behavior.

neglectful-indifferent style of managing children, dis-cussed in chapters three and five

Nelson, Charles A. III; Professor of Pediatrics, Harvard Medical School and Richard David Scott Chair in Pediatric Developmental Medicine Research at Children's Hospital in Boston; w/others (2005). "Attachment in institutionalized and community children in Romania." *Child Development*, 76, 1015–1028 and (2007). "Cognitive recovery in socially deprived young children: The Bucharest early intervention project." *Science*, 318, 1937–1940; **35**

Nemours Foundation; non-profit headquartered in Jack-sonville, Florida, created by philanthropist Alfred I. du Pont in 1936, that's dedicated to improving the health of children. The Foundation operates the

parables of Jesus; **36-37, 126**, also see examples, teaching with

parentese; caregivers' baby talk, **32**

Parents; popular magazine for parents published by the Meredith Corporation, also *American Baby and Family Circle*, **240**

paternity DNA tests in Britain; *The Times*, August 11, 2005, "It's a very testing time for fathers." **67-68**

Patton, George S. III (1885–1945); famed World War-II general, nicknamed "Blood and Guts" for his aggressive battle leadership. "Prepare for the unknown by studying how others in the past have coped with the unforeseeable and the unpredictable." **47**

People's Republic of China's UN mission; NYC, **59-60**

phonemes; initial language sounds indicating possible words, **19, 133**

Pianta, Robert C.; Dean of the Curry School of Education, University of Virginia. Coauthor with M. Stuhlman (2009). "Profiles of educational quality in first grade." *Elementary School Journal 109*(4), 323–342, 34; with Andrew J. Mashburn and others (2008). "Measures of classroom quality in pre-kindergarten and children's development of academic, language, and social skills." *Child Development, 79*(3), 732–749, and with Bridget K. Hamre (2005). "Can instructional and emotional support in the first-grade classroom make a difference for children at risk of school failure," *Child Development, 76*(5), 949–967. Also, Pianta's comments in Malcolm Gladwell's "Most likely to succeed" article, The New Yorker, December 15, 2008. **33-34**

Because the University of Virginia (UV) teams neglect psychological concepts and literature, such as social interaction and attachment, I am troubled by their publications on classroom research, which often include other universities' professors. After repeated inquiries to UV researchers, UV Dean Robert Pianta finally emailed me to say "we use everyday terminology so that educators can more easily understand our work and interpret the findings." I would argue that responsible educators, those who would make the most of their results, don't need to be talked down to. Parents, relatives, and classroom teachers can grasp concepts if they are clearly defined and their use well-described with examples, as I have sought to do in this book. Pedantry isn't the point; it's about seeking process that is unequivocal and interrelation of the new with past knowledge for maximal generalizability. When they say that the best teachers show "more positive emotions and were sensitive to children's needs," what "positive emotions" and sensitivities do they mean? When they say "teacher-pupil interaction," why did they neglect to connect that to the ample literature on social interaction and attachment theories? Superior parenting and teaching are practical sciences that should be steadily expanded and reinforced.

Educational researchers must adhere to the rules of science and be responsible to existing and future knowledge. Pedestrian language can be imprecise and misinterpreted, as was learned from the vague and empty verbiage of the Progressive Education Movement, as discussed in chapter four. Psychology and psychiatry include numerous concepts that are meaningful assets of knowledge that displace everyday language, such as autism, agoraphobia, identity crisis, Type A behavior, need for achievement, etc. The sciences of biology, economics, medicine, physics, etc. would come to a standstill without their proven concepts and complex interrelationships. Minus Newton's theory of gravity, how would everyday language explain that phenomenon and relate it to Einstein's relativity theory? I trust that my interpretation of their findings does not conflict with their meaning. Their journal articles would have greater impact and carry-through to further studies if they had related their research to professional/technical terms and sources. In regards to their targeted audience, their studies have been published in expensive journals that few if any practicing educators would read; for example, the cost for *Child Development* is over $600/year and a download copy of one article costs $29.95.

Finally, I wonder if the UV teams are aware of former UV psychologist Mary Ainsworth, who was a friend of mine. She won many honors and is cited in psychological textbooks for her classic "The Stranger Situation" experiments to describe and define positive and negative attachment.

Planned Parenthood Federation of America; sexual and reproductive health care advocate that works to

is paralyzed except for essential functions, such as breathing. Giant neurons in the brain discharge as fanciful and illogical dreaming occurs. Four or five waves cycle between NREM to REM during eight hours of sleep. NREM fulfills physiological restoration and REM provides psychological restoration. **51-52**

Rapoport, Judith; Chief of the Child Psychiatry Branch, National Institute of Mental Health. With others: (2006). "Dynamic mapping of normal human hippocampal development," *Hippocampus*, *16*(8), 664–672 and (1999). Progressive cortical change during adolescence in childhood-onset schizophrenia: A longitudinal magnetic resonance imaging study, *Archives of General Psychiatry*, *56*, 649-654, **23-24, 25**

Ravitch, Diane; Research Professor of Education, NYU education writer; author of (2010). *The death and life of the great American school system: How testing and choice are undermining education*, and "The myth of charter schools," *The New York Review of Books*. November 11, 2010, **121**

Reagan, Ronald (1911–2004); 40th President. "But there are advantages to being elected President. The day after I was elected, I had my high school grades classified Top Secret." **150**

resource teachers, use of, **115**

Ricci, Matteo (1556–1602); SJ, founded the Jesuit China Mission in 1583, **133**

Richard David Scott Endowment Fund; affords grants for clinical research, **35**

social interaction; major concept of this book that chapter one introduces and other chapters discuss

Socrates (469–399 BC); Greek philosopher known for his Socratic method, a commonly used tool today in discussions and teaching in which questions are asked not only to draw answers, but also to encourage insight into the issue at hand; "Do not do to others what angers you if done to you by others." **30**

Somervell, Robert; English teacher and bursar at Harrow School, who taught young Churchill to write, **200, 203, 211**

Sonoma County Department of Education, **117**

South Korea; population of 48.1 million; Its educational systems rated one of world's best, **218, 219, 222, 226, 227**

split parental alliances, **202**

Stalin, Joseph (1878–1953); ruler of the USSR, **165**

Stand Up for Kids; see Koca

Stanford University, **56, 67, 81, 87, 125, 128, 151, 152, 186, 200, 201**

Stein, Henry T.; Director of the Alfred Adler Institute of San Francisco and Northwestern Washington, **100-103**

Sterne, Laurence (1713–1768); English novelist and Anglican clergyman; best known for the novel: (1759). *The life and opinions of Tristram Shandy, gentleman.* "The desire of knowledge, like the thirst of riches, increases ever with the acquisition of it." **37**